GlassFish Administration

Administer and configure the GlassFish v2
application server

Xuekun Kou

BIRMINGHAM - MUMBAI

GlassFish Administration

Copyright © 2009 Packt Publishing

First published: December 2009

Production Reference: 1081209

Published by Packt Publishing Ltd.
32 Lincoln Road
Olton
Birmingham, B27 6PA, UK.

ISBN 978-1-847196-50-7

www.packtpub.com

Cover Image by Parag Kadam (paragvkadam@gmail.com)

Credits

Author
Xuekun Kou

Reviewers
Dies Köper

Jagadesh Munta

Acquisition Editor
Sarah Cullington

Development Editor
Swapna Verlekar

Technical Editor
Neha Damle

Copy Editor
Sanchari Mukherjee

Indexer
Rekha Nair

Editorial Team Leader
Gagandeep Singh

Project Team Leader
Lata Basantani

Project Coordinator
Joel Goveya

Proofreader
Lesley Harrison

Graphics
Nilesh R. Mohite

Production Coordinator
Adline Swetha Jesuthas

Cover Work
Adline Swetha Jesuthas

About the Author

Xuekun Kou has been architecting, and developing enterprise Java applications since the early days of J2EE. He provides consulting services on Java and Java EE technology, and he also trains architects and developers on the Java technology, software engineering, and enterprise architecture. Xuekun has worked extensively with most of the well-known Java EE application server products, and his experience with GlassFish can be traced back to its ancestors—the iPlanet, Sun ONE, and Sun Java System Application Server series. He earned his Master's degrees from the Florida State University, and his Bachelor's degree from the University of Science and Technology of China.

Acknowledgement

First, I want to thank Packt for giving me the opportunity to write this book. I am grateful to my editors, Sarah Cullington, Swapna Verlekar, Joel Goveya, and everyone else from Packt. Without their encouragement, perseverance and excellent work, it would have been impossible to finish this book.

I also want to acknowledge the following colleagues over the years: Jim Quasius, Bill Nelson, Matt Heimer, Jessica Emmons, Elie Dagher, Peggy Harrington, Michael De Loia, Ron Pinkerton, Tom McGinn, Darren Smith, Jason Mitchell, Joey White, Reid Morrison, Murali Katapali, and Lloyd Fischer. I learned a tremendous amount from working with these excellent people.

Over my seven years of working as a Sun Certified Instructor for the best IT professional training organization, the Sun Learning Services. I was very fortunate to work with and learn from the most knowledgeable and passionate group of Java and Java Enterprise System training specialists. I want to thank every one of them.

Most importantly, I want to thank my family: my parents, Jiren and Hezhi for giving me the best education and teaching me the value of hardwork; my wife, Jianghua, for her unconditional love and support; and my son Jeffrey, for the all the joy he brings to us.

About the Reviewers

Dies Köper has been a member of the development group of Fujitsu's J2EE application server Interstage for eight years. The various roles he took on in the EJB, Servlet, and Web Services teams have given him extensive exposure to the various Java and Java EE technologies. In early 2007, he started looking at GlassFish as a base for Interstage's Java EE 5 container implementation.

He recently moved from Japan to Sydney, Australia, with his wife Emi and is now working as senior software developer for Fujitsu Australia Software Technology, where his main role is to collaborate with the GlassFish developers to make sure improvements of quality and other issues encountered by Fujitsu are applied in GlassFish too.

In early 2009, he was granted committer privileges for the GlassFish project. He has since committed over fifty patches.

Jagadesh Munta has 14 years of IT industry experience. He's been at Sun Microsystems for the last 9 years. Prior to that he had worked in Intelligroup Asia Pvt. Ltd, NRSA (Department of Space) organizations. He currently works with the Software Quality Engineering Group as a lead engineer on the SailFin and GlassFish Application Servers. He's developing test applications for the security module, discovering the use of new tools, developing harnesses, utilities, and improving automation frameworks. He has a MS degree in Software Engineering from San Jose State and a Bachelor of Technology in Computer Science and Engineering from Jawaharlal Nehru Technological University (India).

Sun Microsystems, Inc. (NASDAQ: JAVA) provides network computing infrastructure solutions that include computer systems, software, storage and services. Its core brands include the Java technology platform, the Solaris operating system, MySQL, StorageTek and the UltraSPARC processor.

I would like to thank my parents (Malakondaiah and Narasamma) and my wife (Sreelatha) and my wonderful kid (Lokaranjan), who were always there for me to support. Also, I would like to express my gratitude to my manager at work. Last, but not least, I would like to convey my thanks to Shilpa Dube and Joel Goveya, who helped me in this effort

Table of Contents

Preface

To build a powerful production environment for your Java EE systems, you need a great application server, and the skills to manage it. This book gives you all that you are looking for.

This book will help you gain the necessary skills to install, configure, tune, and troubleshoot GlassFish so that you can fully unleash its power. It will teach you how to use the GlassFish application server, with a special focus on administration tasks. It presents the GlassFish administrative tasks in a logical sequence, with each chapter focusing on a specific topic.

Starting with installation and moving on to configuration, this book takes a careful look at the administration console so that you get a complete understanding of GlassFish and its administrative features. It will help you understand how to deploy Java EE, Ruby on Rails and other supported applications to GlassFish, and how to configure the necessary resources for these applications. You will also learn how to maintain, tune, and troubleshoot your GlassFish Server. Also, it includes a bonus chapter introducing Glassfish v3.

What this book covers

Chapter 1: Getting Started provides a high-level introduction to GlassFish. It also provides a detailed recipe for installing the GlassFish Server, and briefly introduces the Admin Console of GlassFish.

Chapter 2: Understanding the GlassFish Server Architecture provides a detailed discussion of the GlassFish administration infrastructure. It also introduces the tools and utilities used to perform common administrative tasks.

Chapter 3: Managing Applications on GlassFish provides you with an introduction to application management and deployment in GlassFish, and gives you some hands-on experience of working on deploying different types of simple applications.

Chapter 4: Configuring Containers and Essential Services provides you with a clear understanding of the container architecture, and how these containers and services work together to support applications deployed to the GlassFish Server.

Chapter 5: Configuring GlassFish Resources provides you with an introduction to resource management and deployment in GlassFish.

Chapter 6: Configuring JMS Resources provides you with an introduction to configuring JMS resources in GlassFish. This chapter also shows you how to configure the MDB container.

Chapter 7: Securing GlassFish provides an introduction to the GlassFish Server's security features and covers the essential services and capabilities of the GlassFish Server.

Chapter 8: Monitoring GlassFish discusses the monitoring features implemented in GlassFish, and introduces several useful utilities that we can use to further improve our ability to monitor GlassFish.

Chapter 9: Configuring Clusters and High Availability shows you how to configure clusters for the GlassFish Server and use a load balancer to distribute load across the server instances in the cluster.

Chapter 10: Troubleshooting and Tuning GlassFish discusses the troubleshooting and performance tuning aspects of the GlassFish Server and also focuses on several useful tools that help us identify and resolve some very common issues.

Chapter 11: Working with GlassFish 3 provides an overview of the upcoming GlassFish 3. It focuses on the new features of GlassFish 3, how to install and administer GlassFish 3, and how to deploy applications to the server.

What you need for this book

In order to install and run GlassFish, all you need is a computer that runs a well-known operating system, such as Microsoft Windows, Sun Solaris, Open Solaris, Linux, or Mac OSX. You also need to install JDK 5 or 6, which can be downloaded from `http://java.sun.com/javase`. If you want to build and modify the applications provided along with this book, you can download and install the NetBeans IDE, which is available at `http://netbeans.org`.

Who this book is for

If you are a Java EE application developer and architect who builds and deploys Java EE, Ruby on Rails, or other supported applications for the GlassFish Application Server, then this book is for you. This book is also very valuable if you are an administrator responsible for maintaining the GlassFish Server runtime. Basic knowledge of Java EE 5 is assumed but you need not have any previous knowledge of GlassFish. Those who already know the basics of GlassFish will still find this book useful as they will gain knowledge of administration tasks.

Conventions

In this book, you will find a number of styles of text that distinguish between different kinds of information. Here are some examples of these styles, and an explanation of their meaning.

Code words in text are shown as follows: "We can include other contexts through the use of the include directive."

A block of code is set as follows:

```
CREATE TABLE  users (
   userid varchar(10) NOT NULL,
   password varchar(40) DEFAULT NULL,
   PRIMARY KEY (userid)
        );
```

When we wish to draw your attention to a particular part of a code block, the relevant lines or items are set in bold:

```
CREATE TABLE  users (
   userid varchar(10) NOT NULL,
   password varchar(40) DEFAULT NULL,
   PRIMARY KEY (userid)
        );
```

Any command-line input or output is written as follows:

```
# cd $AS_INSTALL/bin
# ./asadmin create-jdbc-resource -connectionpoolid MySQLPool jdbc/DevDS
```

New terms and **important words** are shown in bold. Words that you see on the screen, in menus or dialog boxes for example, appear in the text like this: "clicking the **Next** button moves you to the next screen".

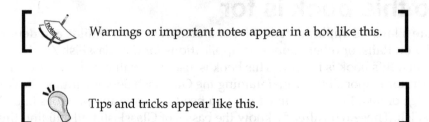

Warnings or important notes appear in a box like this.

Tips and tricks appear like this.

Reader feedback

Feedback from our readers is always welcome. Let us know what you think about this book—what you liked or may have disliked. Reader feedback is important for us to develop titles that you really get the most out of.

To send us general feedback, simply send an email to feedback@packtpub.com, and mention the book title via the subject of your message.

If there is a book that you need and would like to see us publish, please send us a note in the **SUGGEST A TITLE** form on www.packtpub.com or email suggest@packtpub.com.

If there is a topic that you have expertise in and you are interested in either writing or contributing to a book on, see our author guide on www.packtpub.com/authors.

Customer support

Now that you are the proud owner of a Packt book, we have a number of things to help you to get the most from your purchase.

Downloading the example code for the book

Visit http://www.packtpub.com/files/code/6507_Code.zip to directly download the example code.

The downloadable files contain instructions on how to use them.

Errata

Although we have taken every care to ensure the accuracy of our content, mistakes do happen. If you find a mistake in one of our books—maybe a mistake in the text or the code—we would be grateful if you would report this to us. By doing so, you can save other readers from frustration, and help us to improve subsequent versions of this book. If you find any errata, please report them by visiting http://www.packtpub.com/support, selecting your book, clicking on the **let us know** link, and entering the details of your errata. Once your errata are verified, your submission will be accepted and the errata added to any list of existing errata. Any existing errata can be viewed by selecting your title from http://www.packtpub.com/support.

Piracy

Piracy of copyright material on the Internet is an ongoing problem across all media. At Packt, we take the protection of our copyright and licenses very seriously. If you come across any illegal copies of our works, in any form, on the Internet, please provide us with the location address or web site name immediately so that we can pursue a remedy.

Please contact us at copyright@packtpub.com with a link to the suspected pirated material.

We appreciate your help in protecting our authors, and our ability to bring you valuable content.

Questions

You can contact us at questions@packtpub.com if you are having a problem with any aspect of the book, and we will do our best to address it.

1
Getting Started

GlassFish Server has many exciting features which have all contributed to its rapid adoption. In this chapter, we provide a very high level overview of these features without going into a lot of technical detail. We will then describe how to install and update the GlassFish Server. The goal of this chapter is to help you gain a good understanding of the capabilities of GlassFish, install a working server instance, and most importantly, quickly get ready to explore the technical essence of the GlassFish Server in the subsequent chapters.

Introducing GlassFish

As a major step in Sun Microsystems' open source movement, the GlassFish project (`https://glassfish.dev.java.net`) was launched in June 2005, during the Java One conference. The goal of the GlassFish project was to create an open source and production-ready Java EE application server. The **Sun Java System Application Server (SJSAS)** 8.x provided the bulk of code base for GlassFish. Oracle also contributed to GlassFish by donating the code of EclipseLink (originally called TopLink Essentials), a high quality implementation of the **Java Persistence API (JPA)**.

GlassFish was originally licensed under the **Common Development and Distribution License (CDDL)**. It was later updated to allow dual license: CDDL and the **GNU Public License (GPL)** v2 with the **Class Path Exception (CPE)**. This dual license structure allows GlassFish to be both friendly for commercial development (CDDL), and to enjoy the consistence of the Java SE's open source license (GPL).

A brief history of GlassFish

Three main versions of GlassFish Server have been released to date. The first version, GlassFish v1 and its commercially supported version, SJSAS 9.0 Platform Edition were announced at Java One in May 2006. The main goal of the GlassFish v1 was to showcase the improved productivity of developing enterprise applications using the **Java Enterprise Edition (Java EE)** 5 technology. GlassFish v1 also implemented several features geared towards application administration and monitoring. Examples of these features included web service monitoring, call flow analysis, and management rule definitions. However, GlassFish v1 did not support clustering and session failover features that are essential for hosting large-scale, mission-critical applications. Due to this, GlassFish v1 was mostly suitable for department-level deployment and application prototyping. In fact, the release of GlassFish v2 effectively rendered GlassFish v1 obsolete.

GlassFish v2, and the commercially supported SJSAS 9.1 (later renamed to Sun GlassFish Enterprise Server v2) were released in September 2007. The main goals of GlassFish v2 were to improve the performance, add enterprise class features, and further promote ease of development and use of GlassFish.

GlassFish v2 uses the new web service stack implemented in the Metro project (`https://metro.dev.java.net`). GlassFish v2 supports the **Web Service Interoperability Technologies (WSIT)**, a joint effort between Sun and Microsoft to improve the interoperation of web services developed in Java and Microsoft .NET technologies.

GlassFish v2 supports the **Java Business Integration (JBI)** specification, JSR-208. The GlassFish v2 distribution includes a JBI implementation developed in the OpenESB project (`https://open-esb.dev.java.net`). This integration provides a unified installation, administration, and monitoring environment. With excellent support provided by tools such as the NetBeans IDE (`http://www.netbeans.org`), it is very easy to create and deploy composite applications that take advantage of both Java EE and JBI based services and components.

GlassFish v2 also introduced the concept of server usage profiles. A usage profile is characterized by the expected capabilities of an application installation. For each usage profile, the GlassFish Server provides a baseline configuration. The open source GlassFish v2 release supported two profiles. The developer profile is comparable to the Platform Edition of the SJSAS 9, which consumes the least amount of computing resources, and is suitable for development, prototyping, and small-scale deployment. The cluster profile supports the clustering of multiple application server instances and load balancing. The cluster profile also supports in-memory session replication, a light-weight yet very effective approach to improve the availability of the deployment. A third profile, *enterprise* is also supported in the commercially supported enterprise edition of GlassFish. The enterprise profile supports session replication using the **High Availability Database (HADB)**, which further improves the availability of the application server deployment.

To date, the latest production release of the GlassFish Server is version 2.1.1. It is fully capable of hosting mission-critical enterprise applications. This book focuses on the administration and configuration of this version of GlassFish.

The development of GlassFish v3 started back in June 2008. One of the main goals of GlassFish v3 was to produce a production strength reference implementation of Java EE 6. Currently, the Java EE 6 standard is still being finalized. Because of this, there is no feature complete release of GlassFish v3 available yet. However, the GlassFish project has released the prelude and preview distributions of GlassFish v3 to showcase some exciting new features implemented. In this book, we dedicate the last chapter, a pretty long one, to GlassFish v3.

Understanding essential features of GlassFish

Since the project's launch, the GlassFish Server has enjoyed continuous improvement and significant growth. Many factors and features — both technical and non-technical — have contributed to the growing adoption of GlassFish. Let's examine some of them in the following sections.

Strong and active community

The GlassFish project provides an open and structured community for building and improving the GlassFish Server. The functional specifications, design documentation, software builds, and most recent production documentation of GlassFish are all made available through the project website. This allows the design and implementation of GlassFish to be reviewed and tested early and often. Also, the Aquarium Blog at `http://blogs.sun.com/theaquarium` provides up-to-date information about GlassFish. The information includes release announcements, technical meeting and event announcements, and the availability of new resources related to GlassFish.

Over time, the GlassFish community was expanded to cover more than just the GlassFish Server. The GlassFish project now includes a variety of sub-projects. Many of these sub-projects produce the core components for the GlassFish Server such as the Metro web service stack. Also, several sub-projects were launched to develop new products and components that reflect the current state of the enterprise computing.

An example of such a project is Jersey (`https://jersey.dev.java.net`), which provides an implementation of JSR-311: **Java API for RESTful Services (JAX-RS)**. These projects form a strong foundation that assures the continuous improvement of GlassFish.

Judging from the amount of communication that has occurred on the GlassFish forum, e-mail lists, and the large number of times the GlassFish software has been downloaded and installed; the GlassFish project has been very active since its inception. You can find the download tracking and adoption information about GlassFish from sites such as `http://blogs.sun.com/pelegri` and `http://maps.glassfish.org/server`. For example, in May 2009, GlassFish was downloaded more than 680,000 times, including all the distributions (The standalone distribution of the GlassFish Server runtime was downloaded more than 170,000 times). The download count was much higher than that of other popular open source application server products.

Here, we would like to make some brief comments on participating in an open source community. It is a common misconception that the only people contributing to an open source community are those who commit code changes. Actually, posting on discussion forums, sending e-mails to mailing lists, or writing about GlassFish have all helped form a great knowledge base. Such a knowledge base not only allows the GlassFish implementation quality to improve, but also allows more people to get familiar with the product and start using it more quickly.

Developer friendliness

As the reference implementation of the Java EE technologies, the GlassFish Server drives home the main goal of Java EE 5 and 6—ease of development. In addition to implementing the Java EE specifications, GlassFish provides many value-added features that help developers improve their productivity.

For example, GlassFish provides the built-in JAX-WS web service testing capability, which allows developers to quickly test their web service implementation. GlassFish allows applications to be automatically deployed in a development environment, and starting from GlassFish v3, new versions of an application can be deployed without destroying the client session.

GlassFish Server instances can be easily integrated into popular **Integrated Development Environments (IDEs),** such as NetBeans (`http://www.netbeans.org`) and Eclipse (`http://www.eclipse.org`). When you develop Java EE applications, the IDE not only provides excellent support for creating and building components such as EJBs, it also allows developers to define necessary resources such as JDBC connection pools and data sources, and deploy them directly to the GlassFish Server. This feature allows a developer to stay in the development mindset without having to toggle between developing applications and configuring the application server.

Starting from version 3, GlassFish is expanded to provide first-class support for running a variety of popular programming languages and frameworks, such as Ruby on Rails, Groovy and Grails, and PHP. The NetBeans IDE was also updated to provide excellent support for developing applications using these technologies. Together, this allows developers with different technical backgrounds to build applications in the NetBeans IDE, and deploy them to the runtime environment that GlassFish delivers.

High quality implementation

The implementation of GlassFish has been constantly taking advantage of the latest developments in Java technology. Besides always being the first application server to supoprt the latest **Java Development Kit (JDK)** software, GlassFish also incorporates new developments in other related technologies. The development of GlassFish has produced some great components and frameworks that not only form the foundation of the GlassFish Server; they are also used in other products with great success. For example, the Metro project implements the web service stack of GlassFish, because of its excellent performance and interoperability with the Microsoft .NET technology, it is now used as the web service stack implementation in several other leading application server products. Another example is the Grizzly project (`https://grizzly.dev.java.net`). Grizzly implements a highly scalable NIO framework that is used to implement the HTTP connectors in GlassFish. Nowadays, Grizzly is also used to build scalable server applications.

Sophisticated administration capability

The GlassFish Server provides a highly user friendly and complete administration infrastructure that is very rare in open source products. The administration capabilities of the GlassFish Server can be accessed through an intuitive web console, the **command line interface (CLI)**, and **Management Bean (MBeans)** programmatically. These administration utilities are used to deploy applications, configure resources, manage the server, and monitor different aspects of the environment.

Configuration flexibility

GlassFish can be configured to use different components and frameworks. For example, instead of using TopLink Essentials as the **Java Persistence API (JPA)** provider, GlassFish can be configured to use Hibernate. The modular approach of GlassFish v3 further improves the flexibility of GlassFish. You can pick and choose only the modules necessary in your environment, thus, getting a custom-made server platform.

The journey the GlassFish Server has taken to get to its current stage almost mirrors the progress of the enterprise application development. GlassFish started as a proprietary application server that implements the J2EE standards in a monolithic architecture, and evolved into an open source, modular server that is very flexible for customization. While GlassFish continues to deliver a high performance Java EE application server platform, it also supports many new programming languages, frameworks, and technologies that can boost the development productivity significantly. For example, GlassFish can be used with a very lightweight configuration to host database-driven Rails applications; it can also be used with an enterprise-class configuration that provides services such as distributed transaction management.

High performance

Due to the quality of the core components, the performance of GlassFish Server is more than impressive. As the only open source application server that publishes the results of running the popular SPECjAppServer2004 benchmark for Java EE applications, GlassFish produces results that are comparable to or better than leading commercial products. You can get more information about the SPECjAppServer2004 benchmark and published results from the website `http://www.spec.org/jAppServer2004`.

Installing GlassFish

By now, we hope you are very excited about GlassFish, and cannot wait to work with it. In this section, we present the very first thing you need to do hands on—installing the GlassFish Server.

Preparing for the GlassFish installation

Probably the hardest part of installing GlassFish is to prepare for it. For newcomers, this can be quite confusing as there are different distributions of GlassFish available, and the installation instructions can be quite different for each distribution.

We mentioned two distributions of the GlassFish Server: The open source distribution that is supported by the GlassFish community, and the GlassFish Enterprise Server distribution that is commercially supported by Sun Microsystems, Inc. These two distributions essentially contain the same software binaries. However, there are several subtle differences you need to keep in mind, as identified here:

- The sources of the distribution are different. The open source distribution of the GlassFish Server is an executable JAR file we can download from the GlassFish community website (`https://glassfish.dev.java.net/downloads`), while the commercially supported version is either an executable installer file, or a package-based distribution for Solaris and Linux operating systems, and it is available at the Sun download site (`http://www.sun.com/software/products/appsrvr/index.xml`).

- The open source distribution does not support the HADB-based high availability configuration yet. Because of this, if we need this feature, we must install the commercially supported version.

While the community distribution of the GlassFish Server is our primary focus, most, if not all the topics in this book also apply to the GlassFish Enterprise Server in the other distributions. We will also discuss relevant features that are currently available only in the Sun GlassFish Enterprise Server distribution, such as the HADB-based high availability configuration.

Understanding system requirements for GlassFish

The system requirements for GlassFish cover the hardware configuration, operating systems, and JDK 5 or JDK 6.

Hardware wise, GlassFish does not mandate a top-of-line computer system. We have successfully deployed some reasonably sized web applications to GlassFish running on some fairly low-end hardware, with the lowest being a desktop with an 800MHz Pentium IV CPU and 512 MB memory. In order to get a good user experience with GlassFish, your computer should be at least this powerful.

In terms of operating system support, GlassFish is officially supported on the following families:

- **Solaris**: Solaris 10 and OpenSolaris, for both Sparc and x86 platforms.
- **Linux**: Redhat Enterprise Linux 4 and 5, Suse Linux Enterprise Server 10, and Ubuntu Linux 8.0.4.
- **Windows**: Windows XP Professional Service Pack 2, Windows Vista Business Edition, and Windows 2008.
- **MacOS X**: Versions 10.4 and 10.5.

This list is ever growing. In our experience, GlassFish can run on most operating systems that support the JDK 5 and JDK 6, such as FreeBSD. Even though there is no official support for this type of installation, you should be able to find enough community information to either install the binary release, or build GlassFish from source.

Both JDK 5 and JDK 6 are supported for installing and running the GlassFish Server. Based on our experience, we recommend JDK 6 because of the performance improvement and additional tools available in JDK 6. Furthermore, we recommend you set the JAVA_HOME environment variable, and add the path to the Java interpreter command java (typically $JAVA_HOME/bin) to the PATH environment variable.

The next two sections explain the installation process of the GlassFish Server v2.1.

This chapter describes how to install GlassFish v2.1. The installation process of GlassFish v3 is quite different; you can refer to Chapter 11, *Working with GlassFish 3* for more information.

Installing the JAR file distribution

Installing the open source distribution of GlassFish v2.1 is very straight-forward, as described in the following steps:

1. Download the JAR file distribution of GlassFish v2.1 from `https://glassfish.dev.java.net/public/downloadsindex.html` for your target platform. For example, if you wish to install it on a Solaris x86 platform, you need `glassfish-installer-v2.1-b60e-sunos_x86-ml.jar`.

In case you are curious, the ml in the filename stands for "Multiple Language", indicating that the GlassFish distribution has been localized with multiple languages. The GlassFish community does make the English-only non-localized GlassFish releases available, particularly pre-production releases. If you so desire, you can install that version.

2. Enter the following command in a command-line terminal to extract the files:

```
# ./java -Xmx256m -jar installer-v2.1-b60e-windows-ml.jar
```

The -Xmx256m option in the command is used to inform the **Java Virtual Machine (JVM)** to allocate up to 256 MB heap memory. This option is necessary; without it the command throws an "Out of memory" error.

3. Once the Java command starts, a **License Agreement** window appears. You will need to accept the license to continue the installation.

   Notice the checkbox in the window. This option allows the GlassFish Server to automatically check for new updates in the GlassFish update center. We will discuss this feature later in this chapter.

4. Accept the license agreement, and the installation process extracts the content to a directory named `glassfish`, which serves as the root directory of the server installation. You can rename this directory or copy it to a different location. This is helpful if you want to install several instances of the GlassFish Server for testing purposes.

   You should find two XML files, `setup.xml` and `setup-cluster.xml` in the glassfish directory. They are two ANT build script files that allow us to initialize the GlassFish Server instance. The `setup.xml` file provides a developer profile configuration, which uses the minimum amount of system resources but lacks certain capabilities such as server clustering. The `setup-cluster.xml` file provides a cluster profile configuration that supports the clustering services.

   If you want to customize the server installation, you can make changes to these ANT scripts. For example, you may want to change the admin user's password. To do that, you can modify the `value` attribute of following `property` element:

   ```
   <property name="admin.password" value="adminadmin"/>
   ```

   As another example, if you want to change the default server port numbers, you can change the value attribute of properties named `admin.port`, `instance.port`, `https.port`, and so on.

5. From the command line, enter the following commands to initialize the GlassFish Server installation:

   ```
   # cd glassfish
   # chmod +x lib/ant/bin/ant
   # lib/ant/bin/ant -f setup.xml
   ```

   Note that in this case, we are initializing the GlassFish Server using the developer profile. Later in the book, we will learn how GlassFish allows us to upgrade the server profile easily.

   You now have the JAR file-based GlassFish distribution installed. Now, let's see how to install the installer-based distribution, and why it is sometimes worthwhile to follow the seemingly longer and more complicated process to install the installer-based distribution.

Installing the installer-based distribution

To install the installer distribution of GlassFish, complete the following steps:

1. Download the installer-based distribution of GlassFish v2.1 from `http://www.sun.com/software/products/appsrvr/index.xml` for your target platform. For example, if you wish to install it on Solaris x86 platform, you need `sges-2_1-solaris-i586-ml.bin`.

2. On Windows, double-click the file to start the GUI-based installer. If you are using a UNIX-like system, enter the following commands to start the installer:

```
# chmod +x  sges-2_1-solaris-i586-ml.bin
# ./sges-2_1-solaris-i586-ml.bin -savestate install.state
```

3. Once the installer starts, the welcome screen of the GlassFish installer appears, as shown in the following screenshot.

4. Click **Next**. The installer now displays the GlassFish license agreement, as shown in the following screenshot.

5. Accept the terms in the license agreement, and click **Next**.

Now the installer displays the installation directory screen, as shown in the following screenshot. The default installation directory for GlassFish is C:/SUNWappserve on Windows, or $HOME/SUNWappserver, where $HOME is the home directory of the user running the installer.

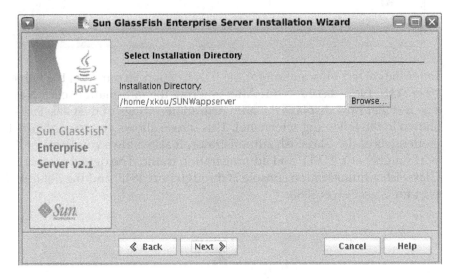

6. Enter the appropriate installation directory, such as `/opt/glassfish` in the Input Directory field, and click **Next**.

7. If the directory does not exist, a new dialog appears and asks you whether to create the directory, as shown in the following screenshot. In this case, click **Create Directory**.

The installer now displays the Java configuration window as shown in the following screenshot:

8. Enter the correct information for the JDK location, in our case, the value is `/usr/lib/jvm/jdk1.6.0_11`. After entering the information, click **Next**. The installer now displays the administration settings of the GlassFish, as shown in the following screenshot. This screen allows you to configure the credentials of the GlassFish administrator. It also allows you to select the port numbers for HTTP and administration traffic. The default access to the GlassFish administration console is through port 4848, and the default HTTP port for GlassFish is 8080.

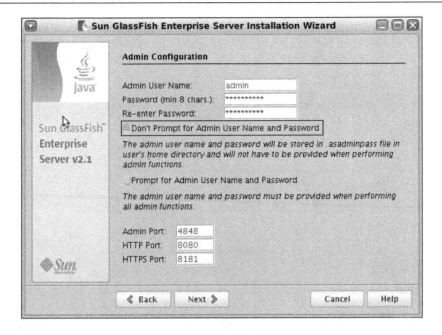

9. Enter a password for the admin user, and select **Don't Prompt for Admin User Name and Password**. Keep the default settings for the port numbers, and click **Next**.

If you opt not to be prompted for the admin username and password, then the encrypted credentials of the admin user will be stored on the filesystem. Make sure you protect this file, so that no one else can read it. Later in the book, we will explain the security implication of this file.

Now the installer should display the update configuration screen, as shown in the following screenshot. This screen allows you to decide if you want to enable the update tool bundled in the distribution, and enable automatic update checking.

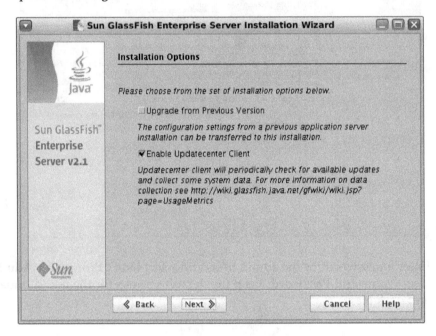

10. Check **Enable Updatecenter Client**, and click **Next**. The **Ready to Install** screen appears, as shown in the following screenshot.

11. Click **Install Now** to start the installation.

   The installation of GlassFish does not take a long time. Once the installation is complete, you should see the registration screen appear, as shown in the following screenshot.

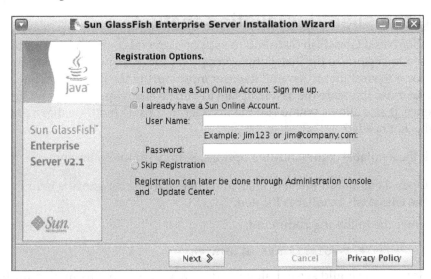

12. Select **Skip Registration**, and click **Next**.

   The **Installation Complete** screen should appear, as shown in the following screenshot. You can click **Finish** to complete the installation.

We will show you how to register the GlassFish installation later in this chapter.

Using the silent installation feature

The installer-based GlassFish distribution supports several command-line options that can be used to customize the installation process for different purposes. For example, you can force the installer to save all the user input during the installation into a "state" file, and later use this state file as a template to initiate silent installations without user interference. It also allows you to run the installer in console mode so that a graphical terminal is not needed.

To check the available command-line options, simply do the following:

1. Open a command line terminal, and change to the directory where the GlassFish installer is located.

2. Enter the following command:

    ```
    # ./sges-2_1-solaris-x86-ml.bin -h
    ```

On Windows, you should see a dialog window with the help information for the installer. On UNIX-like operating systems, the same information is displayed in the terminal window where the command was started.

For example, if you used the -savestate option to run the installer as follows:

```
# ./sges-2_1-solaris-x86-ml.bin -savestate install.state
```

After the installation, you can modify the install.state file to provide some different installation parameters. Following is an example of the state file. As you can see, this property-based text file captures essential information required for installing GlassFish.

```
[STATE_BEGIN Sun GlassFish Enterprise Server f99a6]
defaultInstallDirectory = /home/xkou/SUNWappserver
currentInstallDirectory = /opt/sges
JDK_LOCATION = /usr/jdk/instances/jdk1.6.0
INST_ASADMIN_USERNAME = admin
INST_ASADMIN_PASSWORD = nqbfxnkdghabkygbdpqzvanqzva
INST_MASTER_PASSWORD = plvrdlcijaefpjlodfgiunatrvg
INST_ASADMIN_PORT = 14848
INST_ASWEB_PORT = 18080
INST_HTTPS_PORT = 18181
STORE_ADMIN_AUTH = TRUE
```

```
ADMIN_PASSWORD_ENCRYPTED = TRUE
INST_JMS_PORT = 17676
INST_ORB_PORT = 13700
INST_ORB_SSL_PORT = 3820
INST_ORB_MUTUALAUTH_PORT = 13920
INST_JMX_PORT = 18686
CREATE_DESKTOP_SHORTCUT = FALSE
UPDATE_PATH = FALSE
CREATE_UPDATE_ICON =
CREATE_WINDOWS_SERVICE = FALSE
[STATE_DONE Sun GlassFish Enterprise Server f99a]
```

If necessary, you can change the values captured in this state file before kicking off a silent installation. For example, if you want to change the port numbers, simply modify the port number values in the file. Once you have made the necessary changes to this file, you can quickly install another GlassFish Server instance by entering the following command:

```
# ./sges-2_1-solaris-x86-ml.bin -console -silent install.state
```

Verifying the GlassFish installation

Once the installation is complete, you can verify the GlassFish installation with the following steps:

1. From a command-line terminal, enter the following commands to start the GlassFish Server:

    ```
    # cd glassfish/bin
    ```

    ```
    # ./asadmin start-domain
    ```

    The command-line terminal will display some status information of the server startup. At the end, it should display the following information, indicating the GlassFish Server has started successfully:

    Domain listens on at least the following ports for connections:

    [8080 8181 4848 3700 3820 3920 8686]

    Domain does not support application server clusters and other standalone instances.

2. Open a web browser and point it at `http://localhost:8080`.

Port 8080 is the default HTTP port used by GlassFish to serve normal web applications and content. If the installation is successful, you should see the default page of the GlassFish Server, as shown in the following screenshot.

3. Now try to access the GlassFish administration console by pointing the browser at `http://localhost:4848`.

    By default, port 4848 is used to serve the GlassFish Admin Console web application, which is bundled with the GlassFish Server distribution. Once the **Administration Console** is loaded, you should see the login page, as shown in the following screenshot.

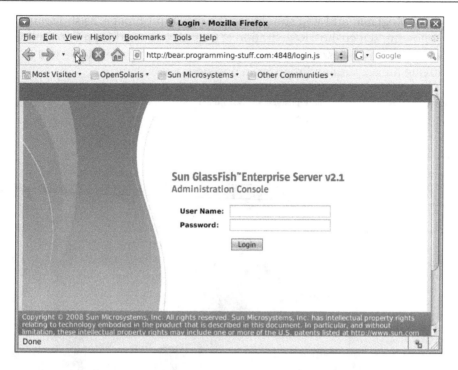

4. Enter the authentication credentials you have specified during installation, and click **Login**.

The default password for the admin user in the JAR file distribution is `adminadmin`. This value is captured in the `setup.xml` and `setup-cluster.xml` files.

5. You should be able to successfully log in to the Admin Console. Its user interface is displayed in the browser window. If you followed the installation steps described earlier in the book, you should also see a dialog that asks you to register your GlassFish installation, as shown in the following screenshot.

The installer-based GlassFish distribution also has a registration screen. If you registered back then, you would not see this dialog here. For a ZIP file based GlassFish distribution, this dialog always appears.

6. Click **Register**, and you should see the registration page, as shown in the following screenshot. Registration is free; all you need is an Sun Online account. If you don't have one yet, the registration page allows you to create the account and register in one step.

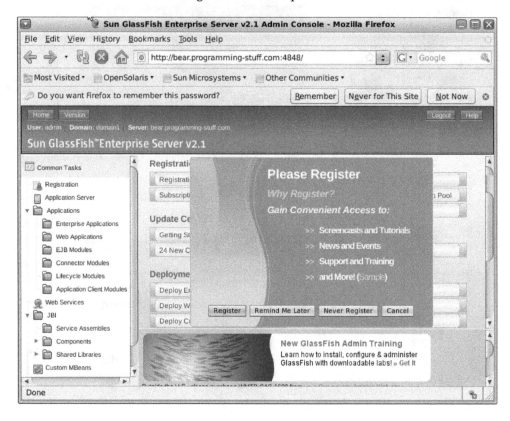

7. If you have a Sun Online account, enter the information. Otherwise, click the **I don't have a Sun Online Account. Sign me up** radio button, and enter the necessary information to create an account.

8. Click the **Register** button at the bottom-right corner of the page to register. Once the registration is complete, the Admin Console application is updated and displayed in the browser, as shown in the following screenshot.

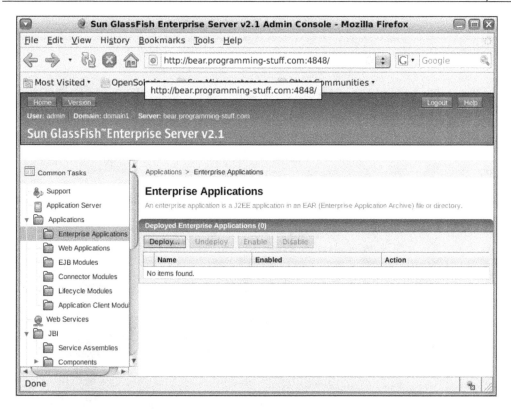

This concludes a detailed walk-through of installing GlassFish and verifying the installation. Next, let's try to explore the directory structure of a GlassFish installation.

Summary

This chapter provides a high-level introduction to GlassFish. It also provides a detailed recipe for installing the GlassFish Server, and briefly introduces the Admin Console of GlassFish. At this point, you should have a clear understanding of the GlassFish Server and its essential features. You should also know how to start the GlassFish Server, and use the GlassFish update tool to manage the modules you need for the GlassFish Server.

With the GlassFish Server installed, the next chapter will dive deep into the administrative infrastructure of GlassFish Server, and explain the most important tools you will use to manage the GlassFish Server.

2
Understanding the GlassFish Server Architecture

In this chapter, we discuss the architecture of GlassFish, and the essential tools we use to administer it. We start with an introduction to the main components of the GlassFish Server, and how their organization is manifested in the configuration files. We then explain the **Java Management Extension (JMX)** based administration infrastructure of GlassFish, and introduce the essential tools we use to administer the GlassFish Server environment. The goal of this chapter is to help you get familiar with the GlassFish administration tools, and the common administrative tasks that you can perform with these tools.

Understanding the architecture of GlassFish

Over time, GlassFish has evolved into a server platform that is much more than the reference implementation of the Java EE specifications. It is now a highly configurable server that is capable of delivering high quality of service. Now, let's understand the main components of GlassFish, and how they are organized to provide a complete server environment. As we see in this section, depending on the usage profile being used, the architecture of GlassFish varies slightly.

GlassFish architecture with the developer profile

If you followed the installation instructions provided in Chapter 1, *Getting Started,* then the GlassFish Server was installed with the developer profile. The developer profile of GlassFish is very light, and its architecture is illustrated in the following figure. Now let's get familiar with the two essential components of GlassFish, the server instance and the administrative domain, shown in the following figure.

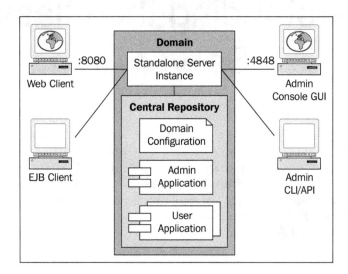

Server instances

A server instance is a GlassFish Server running in a single **Java Virtual Machine (JVM)** process. The server instance implements containers for Java EE components, including the web container for web application modules and EJB container for EJB modules. In addition, the server instance provides the capability necessary for enabling client access and resource management. For example, the HTTP capability of the server instance is based on the Grizzly project (`https://grizzly.dev.java.net`), which provides a Java NIO based HTTP server that is highly scalable.

The server instance hosts enterprise applications and resources. While it is usually sufficient to create a single server instance on a physical host, in certain scenarios, it can be beneficial to create multiple server instances on one physical host for application isolation and rolling upgrades.

GlassFish supports the concept of virtual servers. Multiple virtual servers can be created within a server instance, and we can enable any particular web application module for one or multiple virtual servers. We will discuss virtual servers in detail later in the book. For now, just keep in mind that virtual servers only apply to web application modules.

The server instance is fully Java EE compliant; therefore it always supports all the Java EE 5 component models and services. For example, the EJB container is always part of the server instance even if none of the deployed applications use EJB modules. Due to this, the server instance is sometimes considered heavy, and starting up a server instance could take some time. GlassFish v2 addressed the issue of startup time by starting services only when they are requested for the first time, not when the server starts.

Administrative domains

An administrative domain (or domain) is a group of one or multiple server instances that are administered together. A server instance always belongs to a single domain, and server instances in a single domain can run on different physical hosts. Each domain has one domain administration server, and one or multiple server instances. A domain maintains its own configuration, log files, and application deployment areas. From the administration and configuration perspective, a domain represents a complete GlassFish Server runtime environment, which is responsible for hosting and managing applications and resources.

The architecture of the developer profile

The developer profile of GlassFish uses one standalone server instance in the domain. This server instance is responsible for hosting both the Admin Console application and user level business applications. The separation of the administrative applications and user applications is achieved by using different HTTP connections. By default, user web applications are accessible through port 8080 for plain HTTP, and 8181 for HTTPS. On the other hand, the administrative applications are available through port 4848 for HTTP, or 4949 for HTTPS.

The developer profile of the GlassFish Server does not include the clustering feature. By running only one server instance, the developer profile requires the minimum amount of system resources, while still providing a fully Java EE compliant environment. This makes the developer profile perfect for application development and functional testing.

GlassFish architecture with the clustering profile

It is often desirable to enable the clustering feature of GlassFish in typical production deployment to achieve better system availability, performance, and throughput. The clustering feature of GlassFish is readily available: All you need to do is to install GlassFish using the clustering profile, or update the already installed GlassFish from developer profile to clustering profile.

A typical production deployment of GlassFish Server contains several additional building blocks, as illustrated in the following figure. As you can see, besides administrative domains and server instances, the clustering profile has several additional components. The functional responsibilities of the new components and their relationship are discussed in the following sections.

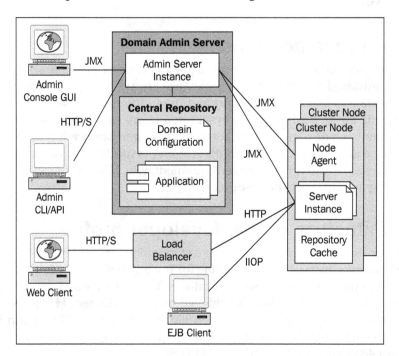

Domain Administration Server (DAS)

The **Domain Administration Server** (**DAS**) of a domain is a special server instance that is typically dedicated to hosting administrative applications, such as the Admin Console web application and other administrative tools. The DAS is responsible for authenticating the administrator, handling administrative requests, and communicating with other server instances in the domain to carry out administrative tasks. All this communication is based on the Java Management Extension (JMX). The administration tools include command-line utilities and the browser-based Administration Console (Admin Console). The GlassFish Server also provides a JMX-based API and ANT tasks for server administration.

The DAS maintains a repository of the configuration and applications deployed to the domain. Each server instance maintains a cached copy of the repository. Because of this, if the DAS is not available, there is no impact on the performance or availability of active server instances. However, in these circumstances, administrative changes cannot be made.

Clusters

A cluster is a named collection of server instances that share the same applications, resources, and configuration information. Typically, a cluster includes server instance members created on different physical hosts to improve the throughput and availability of the server deployment. This is sometimes called horizontal scalability. Server instance members of a cluster are typically configured in a load-balancing strategy to simplify the client's view of the server environment. A client does not need to know the physical location information of individual server instances.

Clusters simplify server administration. A server administrator can easily control the lifecycle of each server instance, and only one configuration needs to be maintained for a cluster. In a cluster environment, when you deploy an application, you do not need to deploy it to each server instance. Instead, deploying the application to a cluster automatically pushes the application to each server instance. Furthermore, in GlassFish, additional capabilities such as session replication and failover can only be achieved by a clustered deployment.

Node agents

A node agent is a lightweight process which runs on every physical host that runs GlassFish Server instances, including the machine that hosts the DAS. The node agent is responsible for the following tasks:

- Creating server instances on the physical host, and initializing the server instance by retrieving the configuration information from the DAS repository.

- Starting, stopping, and restarting server instances as instructed by the DAS or in the event of a server instance failure.

- Providing diagnostic information about the lifecycle change events that occurred to server instances, such as a failure.

- Synchronizing each server instance's local configuration repository with the DAS's central repository.

- Performing appropriate cleanup when a server instance is deleted.

Each physical host must have at least one node agent for each domain to which the host belongs, and the node agent must always be running to control the lifecycle of server instances.

Using the clustering profile

The clustering profile not only allows multiple server instances to be used to provide more server processing power, it also provides several additional advantages. For example, the clustering profile simplifies the configuration of multiple server instances. We only need to maintain one configuration at the cluster level, regardless of how many server instances the cluster contains. Also, application and resource deployment is also easier, because they only need to be deployed to the cluster, and they are automatically deployed to each server instance. Furthermore, the clustering profile provides a light-weight, in-memory session fail over solution to improve the availability of the server environment.

Due to these excellent features, we should consider using GlassFish with the clustering profile in most production environments, and also in environments where system load and stress tests are performed.

Using the enterprise profile

There is a third usage profile supported in GlassFish, that is, *enterprise*. The enterprise profile is quite similar to the clustering profile, wherein it supports all the GlassFish components like domains, server instances, and so on. The differences between clustering and enterprise profiles are mainly in the following areas:

- The enterprise profile uses the **High Availability Database (HADB)** to persist user session date, while the clustering profile essentially uses the server memory to do the same.

- The enterprise profile is not open-source; due to the license structure of HADB, the enterprise profile is not supported in the open source distribution of GlassFish. You can only get this feature by using the commercially supported distribution, the GlassFish Enterprise Server.

The following table highlights the differences of the three usage profiles.

Configuration	Developer	Clustering	Enterprise
Available in open source distribution	Yes	Yes	No
Server resource requirement	Low	High	Very high
Separate DAS	No	Yes	Yes
Use node agent	No	Yes	Yes
Support clustering	No	Yes	Yes
State replication	Not supported	In memory	Database

Now that we understand the main components of GlassFish, let's discuss how they are organized in a physical installation.

Understanding the GlassFish deployment structure

In this section, we will get familiar with the GlassFish Server's overall directory structure, and then dive into the administrative domain to explore the GlassFish configuration files.

The directory structure of GlassFish

The essential directory structure of a GlassFish installation is illustrated in the following screenshot. The purpose and content of these directories are discussed in the following section.

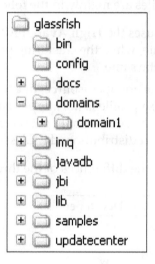

 The installer-based GlassFish distribution also creates several additional directories and files such as the uninstaller. We do not discuss this content in this chapter. You can find more information on them in the GlassFish documentation.

The **bin** directory contains important executable scripts for the GlassFish. For example, the asadmin script is the primary command line (CLI) administrative tools for GlassFish. You have used asadmin to start and stop the GlassFish Server earlier in the chapter, and a detailed discussion of the capability of asadmin will be given in the next chapter.

The **config** directory contains two configuration scripts that define the GlassFish system environment information. For example, the asenv script captures the GlassFish installation environment, such as the location of the JDK software.

The **imq** directory contains the server binary of the OpenMQ software. OpenMQ is a high performance JMS provider, and we will discuss OpenMQ later in this book.

The **jbi** directory contains the **Java Business Integration (JBI)** runtime environment that is integrated with the GlassFish Server.

The directory **javadb** contains a distribution of the Java DB Database system based on the Apache Derby project. Java DB provides a small and pure Java implementation of a **Relational Database System (RDBMS)**. It can be used as an embedded persistent and relational data store. In fact, the GlassFish timer service and call flow monitoring feature both use the embedded Java DB for data storage. Java DB is also suitable for prototyping and small scale deployment.

The **lib** directory contains the system level library files. For example, it contains the GlassFish's runtime library `appserver-rt.jar`, and the Java EE standard libraries, `javaee.jar`. These libraries are loaded by the GlassFish's system class loader to provide the core runtime environment of the GlassFish Server. Furthermore, the **lib** directory also contains a **dtds** sub directory that stores the XML DTD and schema definitions for Java EE, GlassFish deployment descriptors.

Finally, the **updatecenter** directory contains the **updatetool** utility of GlassFish. The other two directories, **docs** and **samples** contain some GlassFish quick start documentation and very simple application samples. The complete GlassFish documentation is available at `http://docs.sun.com/app/docs/prod/gf.ent.svr`, and you can download the Java EE sample and blueprint applications from `http://java.sun.com/javaee`.

The last, and maybe the most important directory for administrators, **domains**, is discussed in the following section.

Understanding Glassfish administrative domains

A domain maintains its own collection of configuration files, security settings, deployed applications, and runtime log files.

Multiple domains can be created for a single GlassFish installation. While this approach may not be very common, it can be very helpful in a hosting environment for the following reasons:

- It is easy to maintain and update a single GlassFish Server installation.
- A domain provides a runtime environment that is independent of other domains. For example, when a domain is shut down, other domains are not affected. You can take advantage of this feature by using a domain to host applications for a separate organization.
- Domains do not share administration information. This allows you to delegate the domain administration responsibilities to different administrators.

When you install GlassFish, a default domain, `domain1` is created. This domain has a single server instance that provides both administrative and application services. In this section, we examine the structure and configuration information of this domain, and get familiar with some of the most important configuration files of GlassFish.

The structure of the default domain

The directory structure of the default domain, **domain1** is illustrated in the following figure.

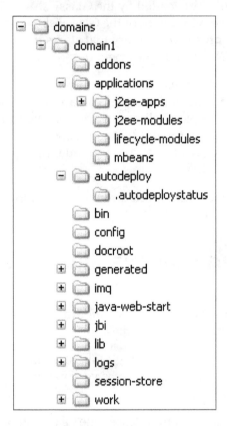

In the screenshot, the directory **domain1** corresponds to the domain root directory for **domain1**. In GlassFish, each domain corresponds to a directory with the same name as the domain. By default, all the domains are created under the domain root directory `$AS_INSTALL/domains`, where `$AS_INSTALL` is the GlassFish installation directory.

The content of each directory under **domain1** is as follows:

- The **applications** directory contains Java EE applications deployed to the GlassFish Server.

- The **autodeploy** directory allows you to automatically deploy applications by simply copying the application archive file to this directory.

- The **lib** directory contains directories that contribute to the common classpath of the domain and applications deployed to it. It also contains an embedded Java DB database that is used as the default data store for the EJB timer service.

- The **config** directory contains all the configuration files for the domain. It is critical to have a good understanding of these files to be able to administer and configure the GlassFish Server.

- The **docroot** directory contains the default static content. Upon installation, there is only one file, index.html representing the default page for GlassFish.

- The **logs** directory contains the GlassFish Server log files.

We will discuss the applications, autodeploy, and **lib** directories in detail in the next chapter, because these directories are highly relevant to applications you deploy to the GlassFish Server. Now, let's examine the **config** directory more closely to get familiar with essential configuration files for the domain.

Exploring essential domain configuration files

The **config** directory contains the following configuration files:

- domain.xml: This is, by far the most important configuration file of the GlassFish Server. It describes the overall configuration structure and information about the domain, and it contains nearly all the settings associated with the domain. Due to this, most of the configuration changes made to the domain will result in an update of this file.

- default-web.xml: This file specifies the default values for parameters not explicitly configured in deployed applications. This file also defines the default web components shipped with the GlassFish Server, and the **Multipurpose Internet Mail Extension (MIME)** type mappings for static content served by the server.

- keyfile and admin-keyfile: These files store the encrypted user passwords for application users and administrators. They provide the default user authentication realms for the GlassFish Server.

- `login.conf`: This file specifies the authentication realms information for the administrative domain.

- `server.policy`: This file specifies the security policies for Application Server components.

- `keystore.jks` and `cacerts.jk`: The `keystore.jks` file stores the server certificate and its private keys, and `cacerts.jks` stores the certificates that are trusted by the server. These two files are related to enabling SSL/TLS and certificate-based authentication for GlassFish.

- `domain-passwords`: This file stores the encrypted passwords used in configuring the domain.

You may see several other files under the **config** directory. For example, the `secure.seed` file contains a secure random seed, and the seed value is reset on each server start. Those files are temporary, and it is very unlikely that you need to work with those files.

Now, let's study the primary configuration file, `domain.xml`.

Getting familiar with domain.xml

The `domain.xml` file captures most of the configuration information about the GlassFish Server. The detailed structure of `domain.xml` is documented in the *GlassFish Server Administration References* located at `http://docs.sun.com/app/docs/doc/820-4338`. This book provides a high-level explanation of essential elements of the `domain.xml` file to help you get familiar with GlassFish Server quickly.

The structure of the `domain.xml` is defined by an XML DTD file defined in the `$AS_INSTALL/lib/dtds/sun-domain_1_x.dtd`. The high level element hierarchy of the `domain.xml` file is illustrated in the following figure. In this figure, unless explicitly noted, the multiplicity of child elements is many. For example, the application element may contain multiple engine elements. The **config** element is highlighted, because of its complexity. The rest of this book more or less focuses on working with the GlassFish Server configuration captured in the **config** element.

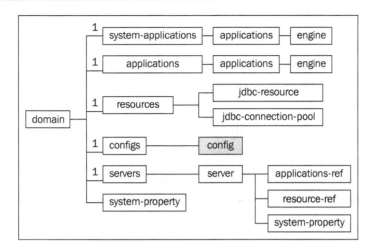

The **root** element of the hierarchy domain defines a GlassFish administrative domain. The top level child elements of domain are described as follows:

- The **applications** elements describe the applications deployed in the GlassFish Server. Typically, system applications are bundled with the GlassFish Server, such as the Admin Console web application. On the other hand, applications you developed and deployed to GlassFish are typically considered as user applications. Each deployed application is described by a distinct **application** element. The engine child element of application is used to specify appropriate sniffers to identify the type of the application, and appropriate containers and services that should be used to run the application.

- The **resources** element describes JDBC resources configured for the domain, including both JDBC connection pools and data sources. We will discuss how you can configure different types of resources later in this book.

- The **configs** element contains one or multiple **config** element. Each **config** element defines a collection of services and other settings. These services together define the behavior of a runtime server instance. The configuration of these services will be covered throughout this book.

- The **servers** element contains one or multiple server elements. Each server element defines a server instance. Each server element contains an attribute that provides a reference to a **config** defined in the domain.xml file. Furthermore, the server element uses its **resources-ref** and **application-ref** elements to identify necessary applications and resources to be supported by the server instance at runtime.

- Finally, the **system-property** element can be applied to **domain, server,** and **config** elements. A **system-property** essentially defines a variable in the corresponding scope (from high to low levels, domain, server or config), and the value of this property can be referenced using the notation $\${prop-name}$. Furthermore, a system property defined at a lower level can overwrite the value defined at a higher level.

As the **domain.xml** file is plain XML, you can edit it using a text editor to make GlassFish Server configuration changes. However, manually modifying the **domain.xml** file is strongly discouraged, because it is too easy to make a typo, which can potentially render the GlassFish Server corrupted. We will see shortly that GlassFish provides several user-friendly tools which can be used to configure the server.

Understanding the administration infrastructure of GlassFish

The administration infrastructure of the GlassFish Server is built on Java Management Extensions (JMX). In this section, we will introduce the JMX technology and then explain how it is related to configuration files in the GlassFish Server.

JMX defines a standard architecture, design patterns, APIs, and the services for application management and monitoring with the Java technology. The high-level architecture of JMX is illustrated in the following figure.

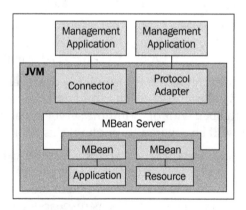

In JMX, applications and resources to be managed are exposed as Java objects known as Managed Beans, or MBeans. These MBeans are registered in a managed object called an **MBean Server**. The MBean server behaves as an agent between management applications and the MBeans. Finally, management applications can communicate with the **MBean Server** with a variety of connectors and protocol adapters.

This figure highlights the architecture of JMX and the relationship among major components: **MBeans**, **MBean Server**, **Connectors**, **Protocol Adapters**, and **Management Applications**.

Support for JMX is built into the Java Virtual Machine. The JVM itself is instrumented heavily with MBeans, and these MBeans are registered in a Platform MBean Server that provides a RMI connector out-of-box. Furthermore, a very useful tool, JConsole, is bundled in JDK 1.5+ releases. Due to this, JMX can be readily applied to managing applications and resources.

The GlassFish Server takes full advantage of the JMX technology. GlassFish provides an **AppServer Management Extensions (AMX)** API to simplify GlassFish management. AMX defines a simplified API for implementing MBeans for configuring and monitoring the GlassFish Server, it also provides a dynamic proxy-based client layer. This allows GlassFish Server to be managed with tools without knowledge of JMX itself, even though you can still access the AMX based MBeans using a JMX-based management application.

AMX defines several types of MBeans, one of them are Configuration MBeans that expose virtually all configurable aspects of the GlassFish Server. In fact, each element in the `domain.xml` is defined by a corresponding AMX MBean interface in the `com.sun.enterprise.config.servicebeans` package. This is actually the reason why the `domain.xml` file no longer needs a DTD to control its structure: the structure is precisely defined by these MBean interfaces.

The AMX API is out of the scope of this book. If you are interested in the details of AMX and other advanced administration features of GlassFish, refer to the GlassFish community website for more information.

Now you have a solid understanding of the administration infrastructure of GlassFish, let's get familiar with the utilities we use to configure, manage, and monitor GlassFish.

Performing administrative tasks

In this section, we will introduce the utilities that help us perform these tasks. Two administrative utilities are shipped with the GlassFish Server:

- The Admin Console: A browser-based tool that allows you to perform administrative tasks using the web interface.

- The asadmin utility: A command-line tool that allows you to perform most administrative tasks from a command terminal.

Both tools can perform similar configuration changes, with the asadmin utility incorporating slightly more functionality. In this chapter, we discuss both of these tools.

Using the GlassFish Admin Console

You have seen the Admin Console in Chapter 1. The user interface of the Admin Console is very intuitive. In this section, we will provide you with a short guided tour around the Admin Console to help you get familiar with its operation features.

Complete the following steps:

1. After starting the GlassFish Server, view the Admin Console by accessing the following URL: http://localhost:4848 in a browser. Enter admin as the username and adminadmin as the password.

   The Admin Console should appear in your browser, as shown in the following screenshot. The Admin Console user interface is composed of the information panel on the top, the navigation panel to the left, and the main content panel. The default content panel displays a page with links to common administrative tasks.

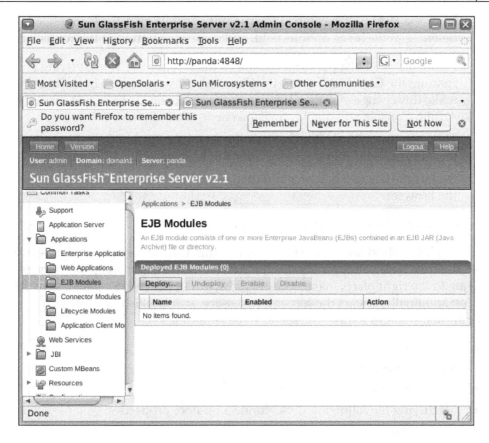

2. Click the **Help** button on the top-right corner of the information panel.

   The context-sensitive help information of the Admin Console should appear in a separate browser window. The help content is also indexed with searching capability.

   This figure displays a screenshot of the Admin Console's help information. The help content contains a lot of helpful information. However, not many people are aware of this.

3. Close the help page browser window, and click the **Application Server** node in the navigation panel of the Admin Console.

   The content panel displays the general information of the GlassFish Server instance, such as the open ports, and the installation directory. You can also click the **Stop Instance** button to shut down the server

4. Click the **JVM Settings** tab in the content panel. Within the **General** sub-tab, delete **-g** in the **javac** options field, and click **Save** button in the content panel.

   As the task you just performed changes the settings of the underlying JVM running the GlassFish Server, the GlassFish Server needs to be restarted to make this change effective. Whenever the server needs to be restarted, the Admin Console will display a visual cue to remind you.

   This screenshot illustrates the situation when the Admin Console reminds the administrator that the server needs to be restarted.

5. Restart the GlassFish Server and then reload the Admin Console in the browser.

The server restart indicator should disappear.

Even though this short tour in the GlassFish Admin Console is very straightforward, it does describe how you typically use the Admin Console to manage the server: Navigate to the right place, make necessary changes in the content panel, save the changes; and finally, restart the server if necessary. In GlassFish, the following configuration changes require the server to be restarted:

- Changing JVM options
- Managing HTTP services
- Modifying thread pool settings
- Modifying the following JDBC connection pool properties:
    - datasource-classname
    - associate-with-thread
    - lazy-connection-association
    - lazy-connection-enlistment
    - JDBC driver vendor-specific properties

- Modifying the following connector connection pool properties:
    - resource-adapter-name
    - connection-definition-name
    - transaction-support
    - associate-with-thread
    - lazy-connection-association
    - lazy-connection-enlistment
    - Vendor-specific properties

Using the administration Command Line Utility (CLI)–asadmin

It is not always desirable to use the Admin Console to manage the GlassFish Server. For example, you may want to create some scripts to run routine maintenance and monitoring, or perform some other repetitive administrative tasks. In this case, using the Admin Console could be fairly time consuming. GlassFish provides a command-line utility — asadmin — that is particularly suitable for these tasks. The asadmin utility is located in the $AS_INSTALL/bin directory. In this section, let's get familiar with the syntax of the utility, and then try to perform some simple administrative tasks.

The syntax of the asadmin utility

You can enter the following command to view the help page of the asadmin utility:

```
# cd $AS_INSTALL/bin
# ./asadmin help | more
```

On Windows, you can run the command asadmin help | help.txt to redirect the help page out to a file and then read the file.

The syntax of running the asadmin utility is as follows:

```
# cd $AS_INSTALL/bin
# ./asadmin <subcommand> <options>* <operand>*
```

By then end of this book, you should be familiar with most, if not all of these commands.

Different commands may have different options and operands, the best way to learn the syntax of each subcommand is by running the following command:

```
# cd $AS_INSTALL/bin
# ./asadmin <subcommand> --help
```

This command displays detailed help information for the subcommand. For example, if you want to know how to run the list-commands subcommand, you can enter the following commands from a terminal:

```
# cd $AS_INSTALL/bin
# ./asadmin list-commands -help |more
```

This output explains the options the subcommand accepts. Many options have a long form and a short form. For example, the long option `--terse` can be written in the form of `-t`.

The `--passwordfile` option does not have a short form. We will discuss this option when we configure security for the GlassFish Server.

Finally, the operand of the `asadmin` command depends on the subcommand you want to run.

Examples of running the asadmin utility

Now, we will go through an example to get more familiar with the `asadmin` utility. Let's create a new domain for our GlassFish installation.

First, try to view the help page of the create-domain subcommand:

```
# cd $AS_INSTALL/bin
# ./asadmin create-domain --help | more
```

When you create a new domain, you should specify the admin server port number (default 4848) and the HTTP service port number (default 8080). Otherwise, if your default domain was not running when the new domain was created, the new domain will use the same default ports, and a port conflict will occur when you try to start both domains.

You can also specify a port base, such as 18080, in the `create-domain` command to force all the ports allocated to the new domain to have a port number higher than the base number.

Now enter the following command:

```
# cd $AS INSTALL/bin
# ./asadmin create-domain --adminport 5858 --instanceport 9090 domain2
```

The command asks you for the admin username. Type **ENTER** to accept the default admin user (anonymous user), and the `asadmin` command should print the following output, indicating the new domain is successfully created:

```
Enter admin user name[Enter to accept default]>
Using port 5858 for Admin.
Using port 9090 for HTTP Instance.
Using default port 7676 for JMS.
Using default port 3700 for IIOP.
Using default port 8181 for HTTP_SSL.
Using default port 3820 for IIOP_SSL.
Using default port 3920 for IIOP_MUTUALAUTH.
```

```
Default port 8686 for JMX_ADMIN is in use. Using 2672
Distinguished Name of the self-signed X.509 Server Certificate
is: [CN=panda.programming-stuff.com,OU=GlassFish,O=Sun
Microsystems,L=Santa Clara,ST=California,C=US]
Domain domain2 created.
```

By default, the new domain, **domain2** is created under the domain root directory `$AS_INSTALL/glassfish/domains`. You can create the new domain in a different domain root directory by providing a `domaindir` option in the `create-domain` command.

After domain2 is created, you can start it by entering the following command:

```
# cd $AS_INSTALL/bin
```

```
# ./asadmin start-domain --adminport 5858 --instanceport 9090 domain2
```

If there are multiple domains within a domain root directory, when you start/stop one of them, you must provide the domain name as the operand in the `asadmin` command.

Summary

This chapter provided a detailed discussion of the GlassFish administration infrastructure. It also introduced the tools and utilities you use to perform common administrative tasks. At this point, you should be very familiar with the Admin Console user interface, and be fairly comfortable with common options and some simple commands of the `asadmin` CLI utility.

In the next chapter, we will learn how we can use the tools introduced in this chapter to manage application deployment in GlassFish. We will also see how GlassFish supports a variety of application types.

.

3

Managing Applications on GlassFish

In this chapter, we will discuss how applications are managed in GlassFish. We will begin the chapter by explaining how different types of applications are supported and deployed on GlassFish. We will then guide you through a tutorial to show you how to deploy and configure the GlassFish Server for several common types of application. The goal of this chapter is to help you get familiar with deploying and managing applications on the GlassFish Server.

Application management on GlassFish

GlassFish provides a server environment which can be used to host a variety of applications. As the Java EE reference implementation, GlassFish is capable of hosting all the Java EE application and component types. In addition, GlassFish also provides an ideal environment to host several popular types of non-Java EE applications. In this section, let's first discuss Java EE application support provided by GlassFish, and then learn how GlassFish supports other types of applications and components.

Java EE applications

As a fully Java EE 5 compliant application server, GlassFish supports all the Java EE application component models, including the following:

- Web components, including Java Servlet, JavaServer Pages, and JavaServer Faces components
- **Enterprise JavaBean (EJB)** components, including Session Beans and **Message-Driven Beans (MDBs)**

- **Java Persistence API (JPA)** entity classes
- Application Client components
- **Java API for XML Web Services (JAX-WS)** web service components
- **Java Connector Architecture (JCA)** resource adapters
- Enterprise applications that provide a single deployment unit of Java EE components

The Java EE standard not only defines the component models and the programming interfaces, it also defines a very standard mechanism for assembling different Java EE components into appropriate modules, and then into complete enterprise application archives. The following list describes the archive types for the different component modules:

- Web components and their dependent resources are assembled into a **Web Archive (WAR)** file.
- Enterprise Java Beans are assembled into EJB **Java Archive (JAR)** files.
- Java EE application clients are assembled into Java Archive files.
- JCA resource adapters are assembled into **Resource Archive (RAR)** files.
- All the Java EE components archives of an enterprise application can be assembled into a single deployment unit, an **Enterprise Archive (EAR)** file.

All the component archive files are created based on the Java Archive (JAR) format. However, each type of component archive has a well-defined standard structure. Furthermore, the component models are described by standard Java EE deployment descriptors and/or Java EE annotations.

Component and enterprise application archives can be created in many different ways, ranging from a manual process involving the Java Archive command, or some very sophisticated process supported in an **Integrated Development Environment (IDE)**. For a detailed discussion on how to develop and create Java EE components and applications, you can refer to many excellent Java EE application development resources, such as the excellent book *Java EE Development Using GlassFish Application Server*, published by *Packt Publishing*.

Non-Java EE based Java applications

Besides standard Java EE applications, GlassFish also supports several other types of Java applications and components.

First, the following two component types are related to extending or customizing the GlassFish Server's capability:

- **Custom MBeans**: GlassFish **Application Management Extension (AMX)** based management bean components that can be used to extend or customize the management feature of GlassFish.

- **Life cycle component modules**: Components that can be used to react on GlassFish Server lifecycle events, such as server start or shutdown.

Next, GlassFish supports some upcoming Java technology standards. A good example is the Java API for RESTful Web Services (JAX-RS). Even though GlassFish Server v2.x does not support it out-of-the-box, as we will see later in this chapter, GlassFish can be extended with the GlassFish update center to support these additional application components. In the case of JAX-RS support, the GlassFish update center contains the implementation of the Jersey project (`https://jersey.dev.java.net`), which provides an excellent implementation for JAX-RS.

Furthermore, GlassFish also supports Open ESB (`https://open-esb.dev.java.net`) components. Coverage of Open ESB and **Java Business Integration (JBI)** is beyond the scope of this book.

Non-Java applications

Through update center, GlassFish also supports very popular applications implemented in programming languages and environments such as JRuby on Rails and Grails.

Ruby, JRuby, and Rails

Ruby is an interpreted, dynamically-typed, object-oriented programming language. It has a simple syntax that allows developers to create applications quickly. Ruby provides a RubyGems packaging utility for customizing a Ruby installation with additional plug-ins.

Rails is a Ruby-based web application framework that has several nice features for rapid development of web applications. At its core, it is a **Model View Controller (MVC)** based framework that takes full advantage of the dynamic feature of the Ruby language to simplify web development. Rails also provides an active record based persistent layer that allows straightforward data access.

The original Ruby interpreter was created using the C programming language. JRuby provides a Java-based implementation of the Ruby interpreter. While retaining the popular characteristics of Ruby, such as dynamic-typing, JRuby is integrated very nicely with the Java platform. Compared to the native Ruby interpreters, the advantages of JRuby include the following:

- JRuby is actually one of the fastest Ruby interpreter implementations.
- JRuby makes the rich set of Java libraries readily available.
- Unlike the native Ruby 1.8, which does not support Unicode for localization, JRuby takes advantage of the Unicode nature of Java characters.
- Unlike the native Ruby 1.8, which is essentially a single threaded interpreter environment, JRuby uses the thread model of the JVM to easily support concurrency.
- JRuby on Rails and GlassFish.

Groovy and Grails

Groovy is another popular programming language developed for the Java Virtual Machine. Similar to Rails, Grails also provides a very productive environment for developing web applications. Grails is written in the Groovy programming language, a dynamic language with a syntax similar to Java. In fact, Groovy can be considered as a super set of the Java Programming language. Grails uses the Spring and Hibernate frameworks to provide the resource configuration and **Object-Relational Mapping (ORM)** support. These features make Grails an attractive option for web developers with a strong Java background.

As we will see later in this chapter, support for Rails and Grails applications is available through the GlassFish update center. GlassFish not only provides a solid runtime environment for Rails and Grails applications, it also provides tools that make the assembling and deployment of these applications very easy.

Now that we have understood a lot of application related concepts, let's move on to see how we can manage these application components on GlassFish. First, let's examine how GlassFish supports application deployment.

Application deployment in GlassFish

In this section, we discuss the application deployment features of GlassFish, and then introduce the tools we use to deploy and configure applications.

Application deployment features of GlassFish

GlassFish also implements several additional features for Java EE applications development and deployment. In the following sections, let's get familiar with several of the most important and useful features.

Automatic deployment

By default, GlassFish supports the automatic deployment of Java EE applications and components. All we need to do is to copy the application archive files to the `$AS_INSTALL/domains/domain1/autodeploy` directory. At runtime, GlassFish Server polls this directory at a default frequency of 2 seconds. Upon finding a new archive, it extracts it to the appropriate directory, loads the application, and makes it available for access.

Dynamic reload

GlassFish also supports dynamic deployment and reload of applications. With dynamic deployment, we do not have to redeploy a component module or application when we change its code or deployment descriptors. For example, when some new classes are compiled, or the deployment descriptors are modified, we can simply copy the changed files into the deployment directory for the module. After this, we can perform a touch command to modify the time stamp of the file `.reload` within the application's root top level directory. For Java EE applications, the application root directory is `$AS_INSTALL/domains/domain1/applications/j2ee-apps/<application-name>`. For Java EE component modules, the root directory is `$AS_INSTALL/domains/domain1/applications/j2ee-modules/<application-name>`. The server checks for changes periodically, and redeploys the module automatically and dynamically with the changes.

The dynamic reloading feature is enabled by default. It is useful in development. However, the periodic change check (the default value is two seconds) can impact the overall server performance. Because of this, in the production environment, this feature should be turned off.

> To configure the automatic deployment and dynamic reload features, we can log on to the Admin Console, click **Application Server** in the navigation panel, and then the **Advanced** tab in the main content panel. This page allows us to enable, disable, and configure other properties for automatic deployment and dynamic reload features.

Directory based deployment

Traditionally, the most common way to deploy a Java EE application is to create an appropriate archive file, such as a WAR file for web applications, and then deploy the archive to the application server. Besides this standard deployment approach, GlassFish also allows us to deploy an application in its exploded directory structure (directory deployment), as long as we specify where the server can load the application from upon deployment.

Directory-based deployment is a feature that improves development productivity. On the other hand, to deploy some applications to a production environment, most organizations follow a formal process. Due to this, we may not want to "short-circuit" the application assembling and deployment process. Furthermore, a standard archive-based deployment strategy always simplifies the job of release management. Therefore, directory-based deployment is rarely used in production.

Enable application clients through Java Web Start

Enterprise application client, or application clients for short, are typically console or GUI-based Java applications that directly interact with the EJBs of an enterprise application. Even though it is possible to build completely standalone Java clients to interact with EJBs, application clients have several advantages. For example, an application client can be managed by the same security configuration defined for the complete application. Furthermore, application clients can always use annotations to inject EJB references directly into its code, so it does not need to use the JNDI lookup to find EJBs.

Unfortunately, the mechanism to deploy and distribute application clients has been extremely application server-specific. For most application server products, it takes a lengthy process to establish the application client runtime environment (sometimes called an application client container) by distributing many runtime library and configuration files to the client machine manually.

GlassFish still supports this manual process for distributing application clients to remote users. It also introduced a very elegant way to achieve the goal by enabling application clients using Java Web Start. When we deploy an enterprise application that contains an application client, or a self-contained application client module upon deploy, GlassFish automatically generates necessary artifacts that allow the application client code and additional runtime artifacts to be downloaded and run through Java Web Start. Once the application client is downloaded to the user's computer, it can start the execution. In addition, Java Web Start automatically checks for updates to the application client, and downloads the new version when it is available.

Java Web Start allows Java EE application clients to be easily distributable to remote users, and it significantly simplifies the maintenance and administration of enterprise applications.

Support Plain Old Java Object (POJO) web service

With JAX-WS, developing Java based web services becomes much easier than JAX-RPC based web services. Java EE allows an JAX-WS web service endpoint implementation to be either web component based, or EJB based. To put it in another way, when we create a Java EE 5 web service, we need to create and deploy a web service as part of either the web container, or EJB container. Again, this process is quite tedious.

GlassFish enables POJO-based service implementation and deployment. Effectively, when we create a JAX-WS web service, we can create a POJO class using JAX-WS annotations, and when we deploy it, all we need is to compile the POJO web service into the auto deploy directory of GlassFish. Just like processing auto-deployed applications, GlassFish automatically loads the POJO service class, and generates all the artifacts to create a web service endpoint.

Configuring application libraries

If multiple application modules require the same libraries, we can factor out these common libraries, store them in a shared directory, and simply refer to the shared libraries when we deploy the application. This feature allows us to reduce the size of application modules and memory footprint of GlassFish, because GlassFish enables the class sharing features for these classes and libraries. Another potential advantage of this feature is that we can update the library of the application without going through complete cycles of build, assemble, and deploy.

To deploy an application with separate library files, we can either use the `-library <path-to-library>` option with the `deploy` command of the asadmin CLI, or specify the path to the library in the application deployment page of the Admin Console.

The main drawback of application-specific library configuration is that this is not a standard approach for deploying Java EE applications.

For a detailed discussion of this topic, please refer to the *GlassFish Enterprise Server 2.1 Application Deployment Guide*, available at `http://docs.sun.com/app/docs/doc/820-4337`.

Application deployment tools in GlassFish

We can use the `asadmin` command-line utility, or the Admin Console to deploy applications.

These two utilities provide comparable capabilities for supporting application deployment.

Using the asadmin CLI utility

The following commands of the `asadmin` utility allow us to manage application deployment:

- `deploy`: Deploy an application module. If the module is already deployed, we can force redeployment by setting the force option to true. We can also deploy a module in an expanded directory structure.

- `redeploy`: Redeploy an application module. Whenever a redeployment is done, the sessions at that transit time become invalid unless we use the `keepSessions=true` property of the `asadmin` redeploy command.

- `undeploy`: Undeploy a web or EJB module.

- `disable`: Immediately disable a web or EJB module. Disabling a web module makes it inaccessible to clients.

- `enable`: Immediately enable a web or EJB module.

- `list-components`: List all deployed modules and their containers.

Using the Admin Console

The application deployment user interface of the Admin Console is shown in the following screenshot.

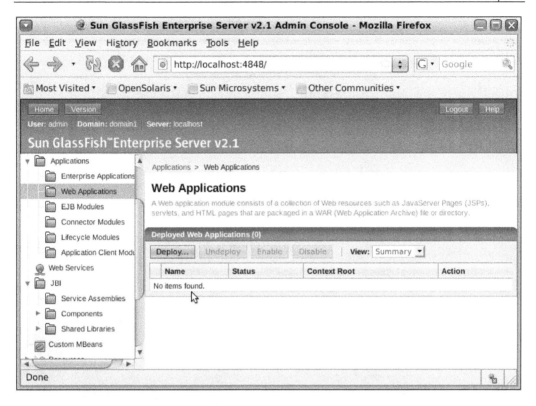

The **Applications** node of the navigation panel in the Admin Console contains the main user interfaces for managing applications deployed to GlassFish. This node has a collection of child node, each corresponding to a type of Java application supported in GlassFish. The user interface for each component or application type is very similar. When we use the Admin Console to deploy an application, click the **Deploy** button in the browser, and provide necessary information about the application. For example, for JSP pages in a web application, we can ask GlassFish to precompile them during deployment. We can also use the `--precompilejsp` option of the `asadmin deploy` command to do this.

Unlike the `asadmin` CLI utility, where applications are deployed with the deploy command regardless of their type, the Admin Console provides the deployment options for each type of Java EE applications. The deployment interface for **Enterprise Applications** is shown in the following screenshot.

In the next section, we will show you how to deploy several simple applications which were created for this book.

Application deployment tutorial

This section shows you how to deploy the following types of application:

- Java EE Web application and JAX-WS web services
- Enterprise applications
- RESTful web services implemented in JAX-RS
- Ruby on Rails applications that runs in JRuby
- Grails applications

Several simple applications are provided to you, and you can locate them in the ch03 directory of the example bundle. All the sample applications provided with this book were developed using the NetBeans IDE. We assume that you are relatively familiar with Java EE applications, such as web components and web services. If you are not familiar with the technical details of these applications, we encourage you to explore the source code of the applications.

Before we go through the tutorial, we first need to update the GlassFish environment to install several additional components.

Updating the GlassFish installation

In order to update the GlassFish installation, complete the following steps:

1. Execute the updatetool script in the $AS_INSTALL/updatecenter/bin. The update center is shown in the following screenshot.

   The update center of the GlassFish Server 2.1 contains many components. These components either extend the GlassFish capability, such as the Jersey implementation of the JAX-RS specification, and Ruby/Groovy support. Some other components in the update center contain some advanced (not commercially supported) configurations. For example, by default GlassFish uses the EclipseLink implementation for the Java Persistence API (JPA).

The update center also provides a Hibernate JPA component that allows us to configure GlassFish's JPA implementation using Hibernate. In this tutorial, we focus on the Jersey, JRuby, and Grails components.

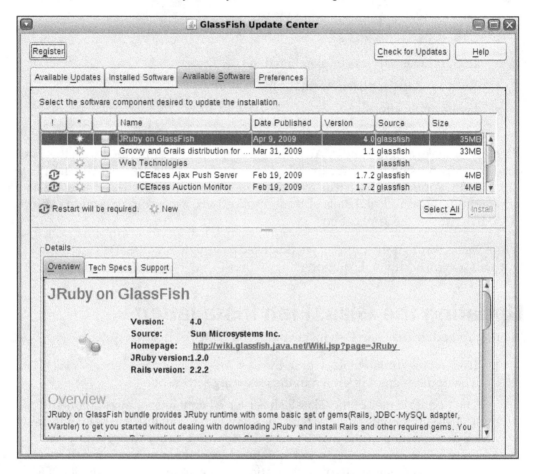

2. Select the following components, and click **Install** to install the available updates:
   - JRuby on GlassFish
   - Groovy and grails for GlassFish
   - Jersey (RESTful Web Services)

3. Once the installation finishes, restart GlassFish.

Now, we have everything necessary to build and deploy applications. In the following tutorials, we will use the command-line interface, and when necessary, we show you the Admin Console interface that allows you to achieve the same goal.

Working with Java EE web applications and web services

In this section, we will show you how to deploy and configure the following simple web applications:

- `SimpleWS`: This web application implements a simple JAX-WS web service endpoint that is consumed by the SimpleWeb application.

- `SimpleWeb`: This web application implements a couple of simple JSP pages to invoke the SimpleWS web service, and renders the event.

- `SimpleRS`: This web application implements a simple RESTful web service implemented in JAX-RS.

Once you have installed Metro, enter the following commands to deploy the application:

```
# cd $AS_INSTALL/bin
# ./asadmin deploy <path-to>/deploy/SimpleWS/dist/SimpleWS.war
# ./asadmin deploy <path-to>/deploy/SimpleWeb/dist/SimpleWeb.war
# ./asadmin deploy <path-to>/deploy/SimpleRS/dist/SimpleRS.war
```

You can verify the deployment of these applications as follows:

For the `SimpleWeb` web service application, you can access the following URL to test it: `http://localhost:8080/SimpleWS/SimpleWSService?Tester`. The tester page has a simple user interface that allows you to provide request parameter values, as shown in the following screenshot.

To verify the `SimpleWeb` application, access the URL `http://localhost:8080/SimpleWeb/webservice.jsp`. The `webservice.jsp` page accepts the user input, and passes the parameter to invoke the SimpleWS web service.

To verify the `SimpleRS` RESTful service, access the URL `http://localhost:8080/SimpleRS/resources/rest`. You should see a simple response like the following:

Hello, this is a RESTful service.

For more information on JAX-WS, and JAX-RS, you can visit the following websites: `https://metro.dev.java.net`, and `https://jersey.dev.java.net`. Also, the Java EE Tutorial book which can be downloaded from Sun Microsystem website `http://java.sun.com/javaee/5/docs/tutorial/doc` provides an excellent introduction to the programming model.

Working with POJO Web Services

Another JAX-WS web service example, POJOWS is provided. This service end point is implemented as a POJO class. To deploy this POJO web service, simply enter the following commands:

```
cd <path-to>/deploy/POJOWS/src/com/programmingstuff/ws

javac -d $AS_INSTALL/domains/domain1/autodeploy POJOWS.java
```

Once the POJO class is compiled and the class file is sent to the autodeploy directory, GlassFish will load it and run it as a web service endpoint. The URL to the web service's WSDL document is

```
http://localhost:8080/POJOWS/POJOWSService?wsdl
```

Once the web service is deployed, you can use the same testing feature available in GlassFish to test this service.

Working with enterprise applications and clients

In this section, we will show you how to deploy and configure the following simple web applications:

- `WeatherApp`: This enterprise application contains two Java EE components — a stateless session bean and an application client.

- `WeatherEJB`: The EJB application module of the `WeatherApp` application that implements a business service.

- `WeatherApp`: The application client module of the `WeatherApp` invokes the session bean in the `WeatherEJB` module.

Once you have installed Metro, enter the following commands to deploy the application:

```
# cd $AS_INSTALL/bin
# ./asadmin deploy <path-to>/deploy/WeatherApp.ear
```

As you can see, enterprise applications have a noticeable difference — enterprise applications are deployed in one unit.

The `WeatherClient` module is enabled for Java Web Start. To access it, either visit the URL: `http://localhost:8080/WeatherApp/WeatherClient` from a browser, or access the application client by entering the following command line:

```
#javaws http://localhost:8080//WeatherApp/WeatherClient
```

> Because this sample application is a console-based application, you should have the Java Console open to see the output. The mechanism of displaying the Java console is platform dependent. For example, on Windows, you can go to Control Panel, then double click the Java icon (called the Java control panel) to configure this. On all the other platforms, you should be able to type the following command to show the Java control panel and configure for the Java console:
>
> **javaws -viewer**

Notice that the application client URL for Java Web Start follows this pattern:

```
http://<host>:<port>/<ApplicationArchive>/<AppClientArchive>
```

If you are deploying an application client module by itself, then the Java Web Start URL would be the following:

```
http://<host>:<port>/<AppClientArchive>
```

Working with JRuby and Rails applications

GlassFish takes the concept of containers beyond Java EE standard, and it supports a variety of very popular non-Java EE application types, such as Ruby on Rails web applications running on JRuby and Grails applications.

By doing this, Rails applications take advantage of the high performance of the Grizzly NIO network framework and the multi-threaded runtime environment of the GlassFish Server. Furthermore, multiple Rails applications can be deployed to one GlassFish Server installation.

The GlassFish Server provides excellent support for running **Ruby on Rails (RoR)** web applications using the JRuby container. This section shows you how to use GlassFish to run RoR applications in GlassFish.

Support for the JRuby on Rails has the following features:

- Rails applications can be deployed to GlassFish as a directory or a Web Archive
- One GlassFish instance can host multiple Rails web applications
- Rails application can be configured to use a thread pool to handle concurrent requests

Now let's see how to support JRuby on Rails applications on GlassFish in this tutorial. We will use a simple JRuby on Rails application to demonstrate how to configure GlassFish. The application is located in `<path-to>/deploy/SimpleRails`.

 The sample application requires a MySQL database backend. In Chapter 5, *Configuring GlassFish Resources*, we will focus on configuring data sources and other resources in details.

Deploying JRuby on Rails application to GlassFish

We can use the JRuby downloaded from the GlassFish update center, or use our own JRuby installation to provide JRuby support on GlassFish. If we are using the version from the update center, then JRuby is installed under `$AS_INSTALL/jruby/jruby-1.2.0`. To install our own copy of JRuby we can download it from `http://jruby.org`, extract the downloaded binaries and install the necessary Ruby Gems using the following commands:

```
# cd $JRUBY_HOME>
# bin/jruby -S gem install rails activerecord-jdbc-adapter activerecord-jdbcmysql-adapter jdbc-mysql warbler
```

Now we are sure that we have a working JRuby installation, let's complete the following steps to enable and deploy Rails applications on GlassFish.

1. Edit `$AS_INSTALL/domains/domain1/config/domain.xml` and add this entry inside element:

   ```
   <java-config>
   <jvm-options>-Djruby.home=$JRUBY_HOME</jvm-options>
   </java-config>
   ```

2. Restart the GlassFish Server.

   Once JRuby is configured, complete the following steps to deploy the sample SimpleRails application.

3. Edit the `database.yml` file in `<path-to>/deploy/SimplRails/config` to point to the MySQL server you can access.

4. Enter the following command to run the database migration:

```
# cd <path-to>/deploy/SimplRails
# $JRUBY_HOME/bin/jruby -S rake db:migrate
```

5. Enter the following command to deploy the application:

```
# cd $AS_INSTALL/bin
# $AS_INSTALL/bin/asadmin deploy SimplRails
```

Once the application is deployed, we can verify it by accessing the URL: `http://localhost:8080/SimpleRails/posts`.

The application's interface is shown in the following screenshot. This simple application allows us to create, edit, and delete post contents.

The aforementioned method performs a directory-based deployment of the Rails application to GlassFish. We can also use the warbler gem to create a self-container WAR file of the application, and deploy the WAR file. To do that, enter the following commands:

```
# cd <sample-dir>/deploy/SimpleRails
# $JRUBY_HOME/bin/jruby -S warble
```

Once the command finishes, the SimpleRails WAR file is created under the SimpleRails application directory. We can deploy this WAR file just like a web application.

Configuring Rails thread pools

One of the biggest advantages of using the JRuby for Rails application is that multiple Rails runtime instances (thread pool) can be created, thus potentially improving the performance and throughput of the application. GlassFish allows us to configure the JRuby runtime environment with the following elements in the GlassFish `domain.xml` configuration file, located in `$AS-INSTALL/glassfish/domains/domain1/config`:

```
<java-config>
<jvm-options>-Djruby.runtime.min=1</jvm-options>
<jvm-options>-Djruby.runtime=2</jvm-options>
<jvm-options>-Djruby.runtime.max=3</jvm-options>
</java-config>
```

The properties of the above elements are explained as follows:

- `-Djruby.runtime=X` sets the initial number of JRuby runtimes that GlassFish starts with. The default value is one. This represents the highest value that GlassFish accepts as minimum runtimes, and the lowest value that GlassFish uses as maximum runtimes.

- `-Djruby.runtime.max=X` sets the maximum number of JRuby runtimes that might be available in the pool. The default value is two. For this element, too high a value might result in OutOfMemory errors, either in the heap or in the PermGen.

- `-Djruby.runtime.min=X` sets the minimum number of JRuby runtimes that will be available in the pool. The default value is one. The pool will always be at least this large, but can be larger than this.

The dynamic runtime pool maintains itself with the minimum number of runtimes possible, to allow consistent and fast runtime access for the requesting application. The pool may take an initial runtime value, but that value is not used after pool creation.

Working with Grails applications

Grails is another popular web application framework written in the Groovy programming language. Grails is similar to Rails. It is also based on MVC architecture, and it also has a persistence layer for object-relational mapping (using the Hibernate open source project). Also, the Groovy programming language is dynamic, and it has a similar syntax with Ruby. However, built as a programming language for the Java Virtual Machine (JVM), the Groovy programming language has a more straightforward integration with the Java language. Because of this, many Java developers have found that the Grails framework has an easier learning path than Rails.

Deploying Grails applications to GlassFish

Traditionally, Grails applications can always be assembled into a WAR file so they can be deployed as a web application. However, the WAR file created was large. GlassFish improved this by taking advantage of the application shared library feature. The following steps demonstrate how to do this.

First, set the environment variables for Grails:

```
# export GRAILS_HOME=$AS_INSTALL/grails-1_1
# export PATH=$GRAILS_HOME/grails:$PATH
```

Now, create the WAR file using the shared-war task:

```
# cd <path-to>/deploy/SimpleGroovy
# grails shared-war
```

Once the command finishes, the file Simplegroovy-0.1.war is created under the application directory.

Now deploy the application:

```
# asadmin deploy --libraries $GRAILS_HOME/lib/glassfish-grails.jar
SimpleGroovy-0.1.war
```

Once the application starts, access the URL: `http://localhost:8080/` `SimpleGroovy/post`. The application should look like the following screenshot:

Summary

This chapter provides you with an introduction to application management and deployment in GlassFish, and it also provides you with some hands-on experience of working on deploying different types of simple applications. By simple applications, we mean those that do not access a lot of external resources, such as transaction services and mail session components. In the next chapter, we will show you how you can manage these resources, and enable them for the applications.

4
Configuring Containers and Essential Services

The GlassFish Server implements a container-based architecture to provide the runtime support for enterprise application components. In this chapter, we will describe the web and EJB containers in GlassFish, and will discuss how to configure these containers and relevant services. The goal of this chapter is to provide you with a clear understanding of the container architecture, and how these containers and services work together to support applications deployed to the GlassFish Server.

Understanding the GlassFish container architecture

Containers provide runtime support for Java EE application components. They also implement the required protocols and mechanisms, so that application components can communicate with the other components and services.

As a fully Java EE compliant GlassFish, GlassFish implements a container-based architecture, as illustrated in the following figure.

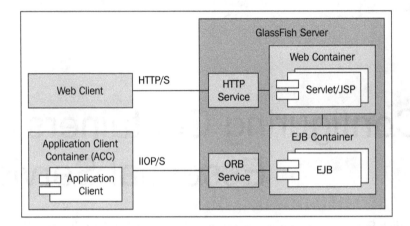

GlassFish implements a web container and an EJB container. The web container provides an environment to run Java servlets and **JavaServer Pages (JSP)** files, and it relies on the HTTP services to allow web components to be accessed through the HTTP and HTTPS protocols. The EJB container is responsible for hosting EJB components, and it uses the ORB service to allow EJB clients to access enterprise beans remotely.

Furthermore, GlassFish also implements a container mechanism for Java EE application clients. This mechanism, called the **Application Client Container (ACC)** can be used to quickly set up a complete runtime environment for Java EE application clients that remotely access EJB components or other resources deployed in GlassFish.

In the following sections, we describe how to configure these containers in detail.

Configuring the web container and HTTP service

In this section, we first describe the configuration of the web container in GlassFish, and then discuss how to configure the HTTP service, which is responsible for enabling the HTTP/S access to the web components hosted by the web container.

Configuring the web container

The web container provides the runtime support for web components, including Java servlets and JSP Pages. Besides providing the standard support such as lifecycle and concurrency management, the web container in GlassFish implements several additional features centered on providing more robust session management.

The easiest way to configure the web container is through the Admin Console. To do this, complete these steps:

1. Log on to the Admin Console.
2. Expand the **Configuration** node in the navigation panel.
3. Click **Web Container**.

The Admin Console user interface for configuring the web container is shown in the following screenshot.

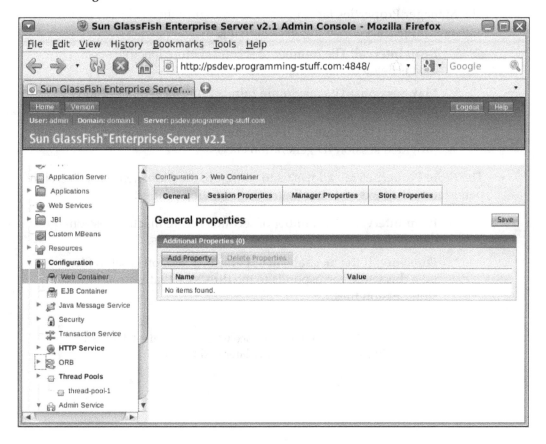

The **General** tab allows us to define some additional properties for the web container. This feature is not used in the current release of GlassFish.

The other three tabs, **Session Properties**, **Manager Properties**, and **Store Properties** are quite useful. They allow us to configure the following aspects of the HTTP sessions.

- The **Session Properties** tab allows us to specify a server-wide HTTP session timeout value. The default value is 30 minutes. This tab also allows us to define additional properties for the sessions. We can define the following two properties: `enableCookies` and `enableURLRewriting`. These two properties both have a default value of `true`, and these properties are used to specify how GlassFish should send the user session ID back to the client. By default, the session ID is both encoded in URLs generated by the server, and stored in a cookie whose name is `jsessionid`. Note that in order to make GlassFish run correctly, at least one of these two properties must be set to `true`.

- The **Manager Properties** tab allows us to configure the HTTP session manager properties, including the following:
  - **Reap Interval**: The number of seconds before inactive session data is deleted.
  - **Max Sessions**: The maximum number of concurrent sessions allowed.
  - **Session ID Generator Class Name**: The name of the user provided session ID generation class.

- The **Store Properties** tab allows us to configure the filesystem-based session persistence. It allows us to configure the following properties:
  - **Reap Interval**: The number of seconds before inactive session data is deleted from the session persistence files.
  - **Directory**: If the mechanism of persisting session is set to file, then this value corresponds to the directory that is used to store session files.

 We will look at session persistence when we discuss GlassFish clustering and high availability later in this book.

We can also use the `list`, `get`, and `set` commands of the `asadmin` CLI utility to configure the web container and session properties. For example, the following commands first list all the configurable elements for HTTP sessions, and then set the session timeout value to 150 minutes:

```
# cd $AS_INSTALL/bin
# ./asadmin list server.session-config.*
# ./asadmin set server.session-config.session-properties.time-in-
seconds=900
```

 When we modify the HTTP session settings for the web container, we must restart the GlassFish Server to make the change effective.

Now let's discuss the service that makes web components accessible for web client — HTTP services.

Configuring HTTP services

HTTP services make the deployed web applications accessible to HTTP clients. The GlassFish Server also supports virtual servers, which allow the same physical server to be treated as multiple logical web servers. In GlassFish, virtual servers are typically used when the server system supports multiple Internet domain names. In this case, a separate virtual server can be defined for each server. The HTTP service can route an HTTP request to a specific virtual server.

HTTP services management tasks include configuring HTTP service, virtual servers, and HTTP listeners.

Configuring the HTTP service

The HTTP service is responsible for defining the overall HTTP request processing settings. To configure the HTTP service using the Admin Console, follow these steps:

1. Log on to the Admin Console.
2. Expand the **Configuration** node in the navigation panel.

3. Click the **HTTP Service** node, as shown in the following screenshot.

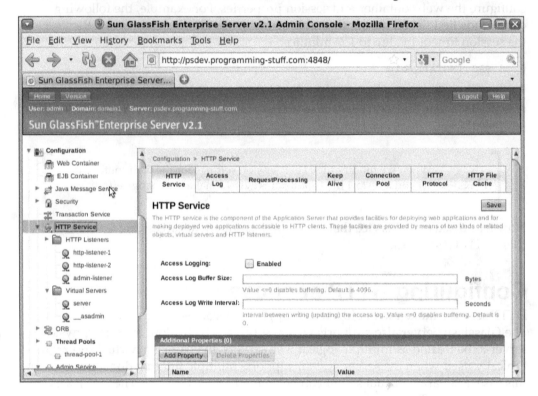

The configurable properties for the HTTP service are described in the following sections.

HTTP service properties

The **HTTP Service** tab allows us to configure the following properties:

- Enable or disable the HTTP access log
- If HTTP access log is enabled, then access log buffer size and logging frequency

The **Access Log** tab allows us to configure the following properties:

- Enable or disable access log file rotation
- Access log file rotation policy (time or size based)
- The rotated access log file suffix syntax and the access log format

The **Request Processing** tab allows us to configure the following properties:

- Request processing thread counts: The initial count, the maximum count, and the increment value. The request process thread count determines how many concurrent requests the GlassFish can handle
- The size of the buffer that the request processing threads use to read the request data

The **Keep Alive** tab allows us to configure the following properties:

- The keep alive thread count
- The maximum number of "Keep Alive" that GlassFish will maintain
- The keep alive connection idle timeout value

The **Connection Pool** tab allows us to configure the following properties:

- Maximum pending client connections
- The connection queue size
- The receive (request) and send (response) buffer size

The **HTTP Protocol** tab allows us to configure the following properties:

- The HTTP version
- Enable/disable client DNS lookup
- Enable/disable SSL for the server
- Content type definitions

The **HTTP File Cache** tab allows us to configure the following properties:

- Enable/disable static file caching
- Static file cache settings

We can also manage these properties using the get, set, and list commands of the asadmin CLI utility. For example, the following commands first look for all the configurable elements of the HTTP service, and then try to retrieve the request processing thread count:

```
# cd $AS_INSTALL/bin
# ./asadmin list server.http-service.*
# ./asadmin get servet.http-service.request-processing.*
```

Configuring virtual servers

A virtual server in GlassFish allows one physical server to be treated as multiple logical web containers, with each one capable of running web applications for different organizations.

For example, suppose you want to host web applications for two Internet domains:

- `www.company1.com`
- `www.company2.com`

To achieve this, follow these steps:

1. First, configure the DNS server or the localhost file to make sure both `www.company1.com` and `www.company2.com` are resolved to the IP address of the physical server (or one of the IP addresses of the multi-homed physical server).
2. Create two virtual servers, and set the `www.company1.com` as the host name of the first virtual server, and `www.company2.com` as the second.
3. While deploying web applications, enable them for the appropriate virtual servers.

GlassFish starts the following default virtual servers automatically:

- `server`: Hosts all user-defined web modules
- `__asadmin`: Hosts all administration-related web modules

To create a new virtual server, follow these steps:

1. Log on to the Admin Console.
2. Expand the **Configuration** node, and then expand the **HTTP Service** node in the navigation panel.
3. Click **Virtual Servers** in the navigation panel.
4. Click **New...** in the content panel.
5. The **New Virtual Server** form is shown in the following screenshot.

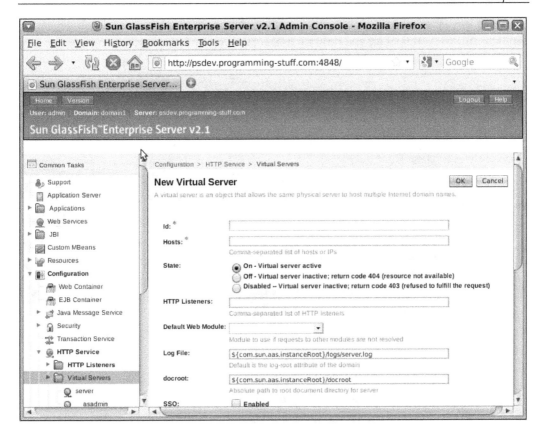

6. Enter a unique ID, and specify the host or the IP address for the virtual server. You can also provide additional information.

7. Once the form is filled, click **OK**.

Once we have created multiple virtual servers, when we deploy a new web application, we can specify the new virtual server to host it, as shown in the following screenshot.

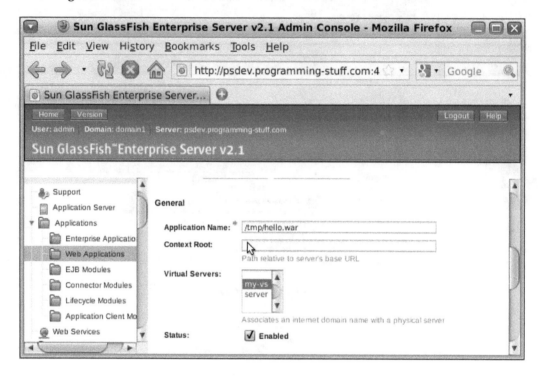

The best use case of virtual servers is for hosting environments where multiple organizations' applications are running on the same server. In this case, creating a virtual server for every organization is a light-weight solution.

By default, a deployed web application is enabled for all the non-admin virtual servers. Also, keep in mind that virtual servers are only for running web applications, and all the web applications hosted by the GlassFish Server run in the same web container. Due to this, virtual servers do not provide complete isolation for web applications. If this is a concern, you can create multiple server instances and designate different server instances to different organizations.

Configuring HTTP listeners

Each virtual server provides connections between the server and clients through one or more HTTP listeners. An HTTP listener is identified by a unique combination of an IP address and a port number. It can also contain additional information such as a server name, a default virtual server, and so on.

GlassFish provides the following default HTTP listeners.

- `http-listener-1`: Associated with virtual server named `server`; does not have security enable. Its properties are shown in the following screenshot:

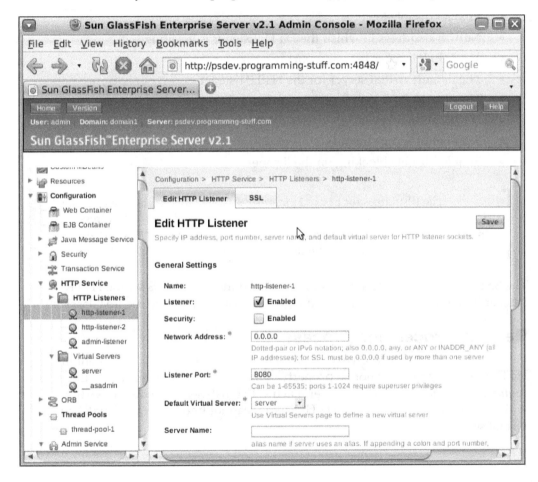

- `http-listener-2`: Associated with virtual server named `server`, and with HTTPS enabled.

- `admin-listener`: Associated with virtual server named __asadmin; does not have security enable.

The configurable properties of HTTP listener are described in the following section.

Configurable properties of the HTTP listener

As shown in the previous screenshot, the **Edit HTTP Listener** tab allows us to configure the following properties:

- Enable/disable the listener
- Enable/disable HTTPS
- Network address to which the HTTP listener is listening
- The HTTP listener listening port
- The default virtual server for the HTTP listener
- The alias of the server which is configured for the HTTP listener
- HTTPS redirect port
- Number of accept threads
- Enable/disable blocking on the listener

> The IP address for `http-listener-1` shown in the above screenshot is 0.0.0.0, which means ANY IP address. By defining the IP address this way, the `http-listener-1` will be used to process any request sent to port 8080 on the hosting system.

The **SSL** tab of the HTTP listener allows us to configure HTTPS for the HTTP listener. Later, in Chapter 7 of this book, we will discuss how to secure GlassFish.

Request processing process

Once the HTTP listener receives a request, it compares the `Host` component in the HTTP request against the `hosts` property of all the virtual servers, and routes the request to the matched virtual server. Each HTTP listener has a default virtual server, which serves as a fallback if the HTTP listener cannot find a precisely matched virtual server.

The HTTP listener's server name is the host name that appears in the URLs the server sends to the client as part of a redirect. This attribute affects URLs that the server automatically generates; it does not affect the URLs for directories and files stored in the server. This name is normally the alias name if the server uses an alias. If a client sends a Host: header, that host name supersedes the HTTP listener's server name value in redirects.

A virtual server must specify an existing HTTP listener, and it cannot specify an HTTP listener that is already being used by another virtual server. Create at least one HTTP listener before creating a new virtual server.

Configuring the EJB containers and ORB

Enterprise Java Beans (EJB components) are Java programming language server components that contain business logic. The EJB container provides local and remote access to enterprise beans.

There are three types of enterprise beans: Session beans, entity beans, and message-driven beans. Session beans represent transient objects and processes and are typically used by a single client. Entity beans represent persistent data, typically maintained in a database. Message-driven beans are used to consume asynchronous messages.

The container is responsible for creating the enterprise bean, binding the enterprise bean to the naming service so other application components can access the enterprise bean. This ensures that only authorized clients have access to the enterprise bean's methods, saving the bean's state to persistent storage, caching the state of the bean, and activating or passivating the bean when necessary. In the next section, let's discuss how to configure the EJB container.

Configuring the EJB container

To configure the EJB Container using the Admin Console, complete the following steps:

1. Log on to the Admin Console.
2. Expand the **Configuration** node in the navigation panel.
3. Click **EJB Container**. The EJB Container configuration page is shown in the following screenshot.

In the next section, we discuss the configurable properties of the EJB container.

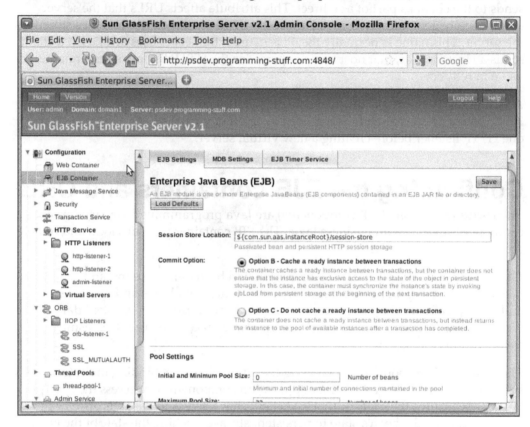

Configurable properties of the EJB container

The **EJB Settings** tab allows us to configure the following properties, as shown in the previous screenshot:

- The location of the file-based session store which is used to save the passivated stateful session EJBs and the HTTP session

- EJB container caching options

- Stateless session EJB instance pooling settings

- Stateful session EJB instance cache settings

The **MDB Settings** tab allows us to configure the MDB instance pooling settings. From a runtime perspective, an MDB instance is similar to a stateless session bean instance; therefore, the configurable properties are almost the same as the instance pooling settings for stateless session beans.

The **EJB Timer Service** tab allows us to configure the EJB Timer Service.

Configuring the Object Request Broker (ORB)

The **Object Request Broker (ORB)** provides the required infrastructure to identify and locate objects, handle connection management, deliver data, and request communication.

Instead, the object makes requests through a remote stub to the ORB running on the local machine. The local ORB then passes the request to an ORB on the other machine using the **Internet Inter-Orb Protocol (IIOP)**. The remote ORB then locates the appropriate object, processes the request, and returns the results.

IIOP can be used as a **Remote Method Invocation** (**RMI**) protocol by applications or objects using RMI-IIOP. Remote clients of enterprise beans (EJB modules) communicate with the GlassFish through RMI-IIOP.

To configure the ORB using the Admin Console, complete the following steps:

1. Log on to the Admin Console.
2. Expand the **Configuration** node in the navigation panel.
3. Click **ORB**. The ORB configuration page is shown in the following screenshot.

The ORB does not have many configurable properties except the following:

- Thread ID: The ID of the thread pool used to process ORB requests
- The maximum fragment size of the messages
- The allowed number of connections
- Whether IIOP client authentication is required

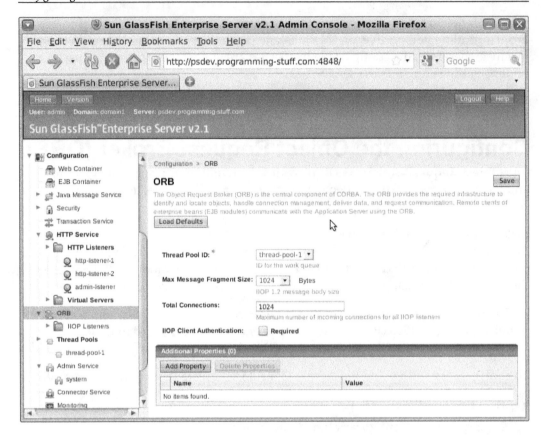

Configuring the IIOP listener

An IIOP listener is a listening socket that accepts incoming connections from the remote clients of enterprise beans and from other CORBA-based clients. Multiple IIOP listeners can be configured for the GlassFish. For each listener, specify a port number, a network address, and optionally, security attributes.

To create, edit and delete IIOP listeners, click the **Configuration** tab in the Admin Console. Click the ORB tab corresponding to the instance you want to configure. Select the **IIOP Listeners** tab.

A **Common Object Request Broker Architecture** (**CORBA**) object makes requests through a remote stub to the Object Request Broker (ORB) running on the local machine. The local ORB then passes the request to an ORB on the other machine using the Internet Inter-Orb Protocol (IIOP). The remote ORB then locates the appropriate object, processes the request, and returns the results.

IIOP can be used as a Remote Method Invocation, or RMI, protocol by applications or objects using RMI-IIOP. Remote clients of enterprise beans (EJB modules) communicate with GlassFish through RMI-IIOP.

To configure the IIOP listener using the Admin Console, complete the following steps:

- Log on to the Admin Console.
- Expand the **Configuration** node in the navigation panel.
- Click **ORB**. The **IIOP Listener** configuration page is shown in the following screenshot.

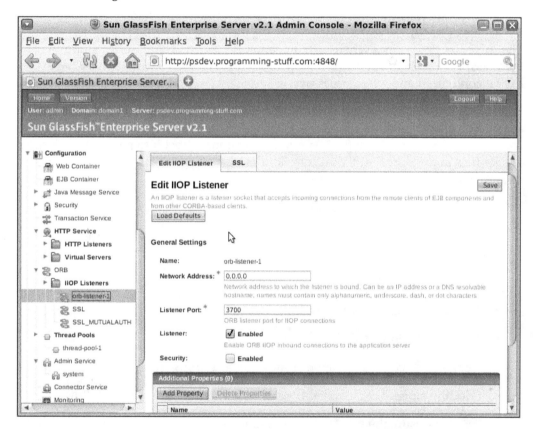

The configurable properties of the IIOP listeners are as follows:

- Network Address
- Listening Port
- Disable/enable the listener
- Disable/enable SSL for the listener

Configuring the Application Client Container (ACC)

GlassFish supports the **Application Client Container** (**ACC**). The ACC includes required Java libraries and resources that can be distributed with Java client programs to a different Java Virtual Machine. The ACC manages the execution of Java EE application client components (application clients), which are used to access a variety of Java EE services (such as JMS resources, EJB components, web services, security, and so on).

The ACC communicates with the GlassFish using RMI-IIOP protocol and manages the details of RMI-IIOP communication using the client ORB that is bundled with it. The ACC also determines when authentication is needed. The ACC integrates with the GlassFish's authentication system. It also supports **SSL** (**Secure Socket Layer**)/IIOP if configured and when necessary.

The `package-appclient` command bundled in GlassFish can be used to pack the application client container libraries and jar files into an `appclient.jar` file. After copying the `appclient.jar` file to a remote location, extract it to get a set of libraries and jar files in the `appclient` directory, and modify `<appclient_install_dir>/config/asenv.conf` (`asenv.bat` for Windows) as follows:

- Set `AS_WEBSERVICES_LIB` to `<appclient_install_dir>/lib`

- Set `AS_NSS` to `<appclient_install_dir>/lib` (`<appclient_install_dir>\bin` for Windows)

- Set `AS_IMQ_LIB` to `<appclient_install_dir>/imq/lib`

- Set `AS_INSTALL` to `<appclient_install_dir>`

- Set `AS_JAVA` to your JDK 1.5 home directory

- Set `AS_ACC_CONFIG` to `<appclient_install_dir>/config/sun-acc.xml`

- Modify `<appclient_install_dir>/config/sun-acc.xml` as follows:

  ○ Ensure the `DOCTYPE` file references `<appclient_install_dir>/lib/dtds`

  ○ Ensure that target-server `address` attribute references the server machine

  ○ Ensure that target-server `port` attribute references the ORB port on the remote machine

- ∘ Ensure that `log-service` references a log file; if the user wants to put log messages to a log file

- Modify `<appclient_install_dir>/bin/appclient` (`appclient.bat` for Windows) as follows:

  - ∘ Change token `$CONFIG_HOME` to `<appclient_install_dir>/config`

To use the newly installed application client container, we need to do the following:

- Obtain the application client stubs for your target application, for example, `yourClientStub.jar`

- Execute the `appclient` utility: `appclient -client yourClientStub.jar`

Summary

This chapter provides you with an introduction to containers implemented in GlassFish, and how to configure them. At this point, you should have a good understanding of the roles of the containers, and some of the main configurable properties. In the next chapter, we will discuss another important capability of GlassFish: managing resources.

5
Configuring GlassFish Resources

In this chapter, we will discuss how to configure common resources in GlassFish. We will begin the chapter by describing resource types supported in GlassFish, and we will then discuss how to configure these resources. The goal of this chapter is to help you get familiar with steps you must take to make these resources available to application components deployed to GlassFish.

Nearly all the enterprise applications depend on one or multiple external resources, such as a database or messaging system. Due to the variety of resource types and features, successfully enabling resource access and integration has been one of the more challenging and tedious tasks.

Java EE has taken a significant step forward in simplifying resource integration. Java EE standardizes the APIs used for resources, such as JDBC. It also decouples the configuration of these resources from accessing them. A resource can be pre-configured in an application server, and made readily available for applications.

GlassFish provides support for the following standard resource types:

- JDBC resources
- **Java Connector Architecture (JCA)** resources
- JavaMail Sessions
- Custom JNDI resources
- **Java Message Service (JMS)** resources

In this chapter, we focus on the first four types of resources. The configuration of JMS resources will be discussed in a separate chapter.

Before we dive into the details of managing these resources, let's discuss one of the most important resource enabling mechanisms in Java EE — the naming service.

Working with the naming service

A critical component of facilitating resource access is a naming service. A *naming service* provider, such as a **Lightweight Directory Access Protocol (LDAP)** server allows resources to be registered within a registry, and later discovered and retrieved by a client. The **Java Naming and Directory Interface (JNDI)** service provides a unified API to access the underlying naming service provider. JNDI provides a naming context as an abstraction of the underlying naming registry.

GlassFish implements a built-in naming environment (known as a naming context). Upon server startup, GlassFish loads all the resource definitions in the configuration file, `domain.xml`, and registers their names in the naming context. This context object also provides methods for managing the name bindings.

GlassFish provides a JNDI browsing facility in the Admin Console to quickly browse all the entries registered in the naming service. To use this feature, follow these steps:

- Log on to the Admin Console.
- Click the **Application Server** node in the navigation panel.
- Click the **General** tab in the main content panel, and then click **JNDI Browsing**.
- The pop-up browser window should display the JNDI names registered in the naming service, as shown in the following screenshot.

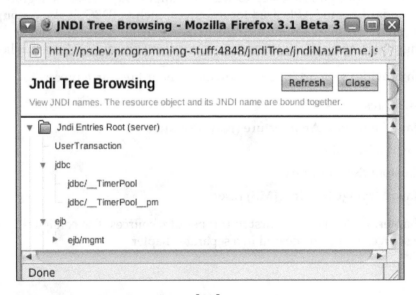

The `list-jndi-entries` command of the `asadmin` CLI utility provides the same capability. It lists the name and the type (implementation class) of the resource.

As we can see in the screenshot, the JNDI naming entries are typically organized hierarchically based on the type of resources the names correspond to. For example, JDBC resources names are typically prefixed with `jdbc`. Even though it is not mandatory to follow this convention, there is no reason whatsoever to break it when we specify the name of a resource that we will deploy.

Naming references and binding information

For applications that access different types of resources, they are coded against a resource reference. A resource reference can be defined either in the deployment descriptor, or by the `name` attribute in a resource annotation. This resource reference can be considered as a logical alias within an application that can be used to reference the resource. On the other hand, the JNDI name of a resource can be considered as the physical name of a resource within the application server. When an application is deployed, the resource reference value is mapped to a physical JNDI name. The following figure uses a web application example to illustrate this mechanism.

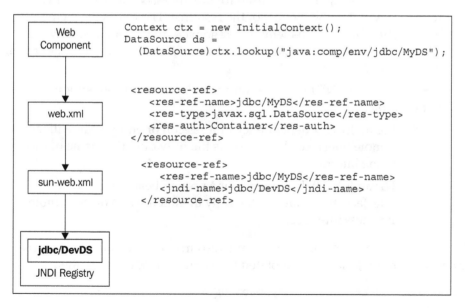

As shown in this figure, a web component uses the local name `java:comp/env/jdbc/MyDS` to lookup a JDBC data source. This name is valid because the name `jdbc/MyDS` is declared in the deployment descriptor `web.xml` as a resource reference name. The GlassFish-specific deployment descriptor `sun-web.xml` resolves (maps) the name `jdbc/MyDS` to the physical JNDI name of the registered data source — `jdbc/DevDS`. Through this mapping, the web component's lookup for the data source results in a data source object becoming available to use.

This approach simplifies the development of Java EE applications, because during development time, developers do not have to know the physical names of resources. This is a very useful feature for large environment. However, it is cumbersome to have to configure this resource reference to JNDI name mapping for every application, even trivial ones. Java EE 5 simplifies this by providing several shortcuts that are similar to the "convention over configuration" approach that was made popular by the Rails framework:

- If a resource is made available to the application through dependency injection, the reference's JNDI name can be used as the `mappedName` attribute of the `Resource` annotation. In this case, the application does not need to maintain a resource reference and its mapping to the JNDI name.

- Inside the standard deployment descriptor, such as `ejb-jar.xml`, the `mapped-name` element can be used to directly associate the resource reference with the JNDI name of the resource. The following elements have mapped-name sub-elements: `resource-ref`, `resource-env-ref`, `ejb-ref`, `message-destination`, `message-destination-ref`, `session`, `message-driven`, and `entity`.

- Assign a default JNDI name to components based on conventions. For example:
    - For an EJB 2.x dependency or a session or entity bean with a remote interface, the default is the fully qualified name of the home interface.
    - For an EJB 3.0 dependency or a session bean with a remote interface, the default is the fully qualified name of the remote business interface.

In the previous example, to obtain the same resource described in the example, a servlet can simply declare an annotated `DataSource` resource like this:

```
@Resource (name="jdbc/MyDS", mappedName="jdbc/DevDS")
DataSource ds;
```

The `name` attribute of the `Resource` annotation eliminates the need to declare the resource reference in `web.xml`, while the `mappedName` attribute serves the same purpose as the `jndi-name` element in `sun-web.xml`.

JDBC connection pools and data sources

Relational databases are by far the most widely used resources in enterprise applications. Besides supporting the JDBC API, Java EE further simplifies the configuration and management of database resources.

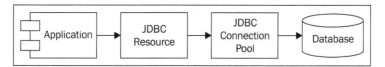

At runtime, the following sequence occurs when an application connects to a database:

- The application gets the JDBC resource (data source) associated with the database by making a call through the JNDI API. Using the JNDI name of the resource, the naming service locates the JDBC resource. Each JDBC resource specifies a connection pool.

- Using the JDBC resource, the application gets a database connection. GlassFish Server retrieves a physical connection from the connection pool that corresponds to the database. The pool defines connection attributes such as the database name (URL), username, and password.

- Once the database connection is obtained, the application can read, modify, and add data to the database by making calls to the JDBC API. The JDBC driver translates the application's JDBC calls into the protocol of the database server.

- When the application has finished accessing the database, the application closes the connection and returns the connection to the connection pool.

The steps necessary to enable JDBC access for Java EE applications include:

- Install the JDBC driver
- Create a connection pool for the physical database
- Create a JDBC resource using the connection pool
- Enable the JDBC resource in the application

The following sections show in detail, how we can complete these configuration steps in GlassFish.

Installing the JDBC driver

In order to create JDBC resources, appropriate JDBC drivers must be available for GlassFish. The open source version of the GlassFish Server is bundled with the Java DB database and JDBC driver. Java DB is the Sun-supported distribution of the Apache Derby database, and it is very good for development purposes. Furthermore, the `asadmin` CLI also has two commands, `start-database` and `stop-database` that can be used to quickly start and stop the bundled Java DB database server. Please refer to the Java DB documentation, located at `http://developers.sun.com/javadb/reference/docs` for more information about Java DB.

In addition to Java DB, the enterprise edition of the GlassFish Server is also bundled with officially supported JDBC drivers, which are listed in the *GlassFish Server Administration Guide* (`http://docs.sun.com/app/docs/doc/820-4335`).

Don't lose sleep if the JDBC driver you need to use is not in the list. Most of the commonly used JDBC drivers, such as the Postgre SQL's driver or Microsoft SQL Server JDBC driver can be used in GlassFish without a problem. This list more or less only reflects how many official tests were conducted by Sun for a particular driver implementation.

To install our own JDBC driver for GlassFish, all we need to do is to copy the JDBC driver JAR file to the `$AS_INSTALL/domains/domain1/lib` directory, and restart GlassFish. The common class loader of the GlassFish Server loads the driver, and makes it available for all the application modules deployed to the domain.

 We can also copy the JDBC driver JAR file to the `$AS_INSTALL/domains/domain1/lib/ext` directory, and restart GlassFish. In GlassFish, this directory is used by the JVM bootstrap class loader to load optional packages (also known as standard extensions) on the JVM startup. This mechanism is typically used to extend the standard capability of the core runtime platform. Because of this, it is not recommended to deploy JDBC drivers this way. For more information on the extension mechanism, refer to its official documentation: `http://java.sun.com/javase/6/docs/technotes/guides/extensions`.

Creating and configuring JDBC connection pools

Due to the high overhead involved in database connection creation, all the enterprise computing technologies use the technique of connection pooling. By maintaining a group of live connections, and assigning available connections to application requests, the system performance and scalability can improve significantly.

JDBC connection pools can be created using the Admin Console or the `asadmin` CLI. To create a JDBC connection pool using the Admin Console, complete the following steps:

- Log on to the Admin Console.
- In the navigation panel, expand the **Resources** and **JDBC** node, and click **Connection Pools**.
- Click **New** in the main content panel.

The JDBC connection pool creation interface has two steps. The first step gathers the information about the name, resource type used for the connection pool, and optionally the vendor for the database product.

The second step gathers a lot more information about the connection pool. At a minimum, you need to provide enough information in the **Additional Properties** section (as shown in the following screenshot) so that the connection pool can be created.

> The additional properties template of the connection pool varies, depending on the type of the database. The most common properties are the database URL, username, and password. For detailed information on the connection pool properties settings, refer to the GlassFish Server Administration Guide.

Once you have finished providing the information, click **Finish** to create the connection pool.

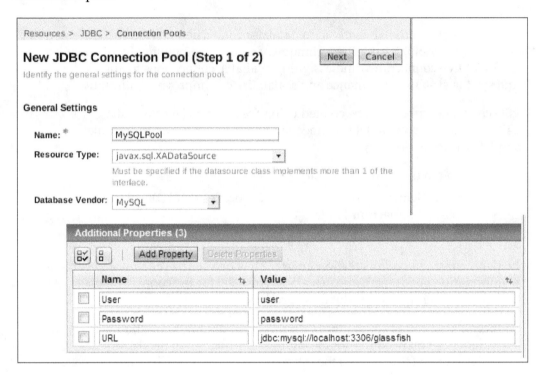

The following example command creates a JDBC connection pool named **MySQLPool** in the server using the asadmin CLI:

```
# cd $AS_INSTALL/bin

# ./asadmin create-jdbc-connection-pool --datasourceclassname com.mysql.
jdbc.jdbc2.optional.MysqlXADataSource  --restype javax.sql.XADataSource
--property portNumber=3306:password=password:user=userP:serverName=localh
ost:databaseName=InfoDB MySQLPool
```

The Admin Console provides a feature to test the connection pool. To use this feature, click the target connection pool in the navigation panel, and click **Ping** in the main content panel. The **Ping** command tries to use the provided information for the connection pool to verify that GlassFish can indeed connect to the database successfully.

The ping-connection-pool command of the asadmin CLI performs the same functionality.

Working with connection pool settings

JDBC connection pools have many properties. Setting these properties differently can impact the system performance and robustness. In this section, we briefly discuss several essential properties. Please refer to the GlassFish Server Administration Guide for detailed information.

- **Initial and minimum pool size**: The minimum number of connections in the pool. This value also determines the number of connections placed in the pool when the pool is first created.

- **Maximum pool size**: The maximum number of connections in the pool.

- **Pool resize quantity**: When the pool scales up and scales down towards the maximum and minimum pool sizes respectively, it is resized in batches. This value determines the number of connections in the batch.

- **Idle timeout**: The maximum time in seconds that a connection can remain idle in the pool. After this time expires, the connection is removed from the pool.

- **Max wait time**: The amount of time the application requesting a connection will wait before getting a connection timeout. As the default wait time is long, the application might appear to hang indefinitely.

- **Connection validation**: Select the required checkbox to enable connection validation.

- **Validation method**: The application server can validate database connections in three ways: auto-commit, metadata, and table.

Creating JDBC resources

A JDBC resource (data source) provides applications with a means of connecting to a database. Typically, the administrator creates a JDBC resource for each database accessed by the applications deployed in a domain. (However, more than one JDBC resource can be created for a database.)

When creating a JDBC resource, you must identify the following:

- The JNDI name. By convention, the name begins with the `jdbc/` string. For example, `jdbc/DevDS`.

- Select a connection pool to be associated with the new JDBC resource.

- Specify the settings for the resource.

- Identify the targets (clusters and standalone server instance) on which the resource is available.
- Specify the connection pool with which it is associated. Multiple JDBC resources can specify a single connection pool.

The `create-jdbc-resource` command of the `asadmin` CLI can be used to create a JDBC resource, for example,

```
# cd $AS_INSTALL/bin
# ./asadmin create-jdbc-resource -connectionpoolid MySQLPool jdbc/DevDS
```

Creating a JDBC resource is a dynamic event and does not require server restart.

Connector resources

A connector module is a Java EE connector architecture resource adapter component that enables applications to interact with **Enterprise Information Systems (EISs)**, such as **Enterprise Resource Planning (ERP)** and some messaging system. In fact, GlassFish provides a connector resource adapter for JMS resources, it allows a JMS-compliant messaging system to be easily integrated into the GlassFish Server.

Furthermore, Java EE now allows a message-driven bean to be defined for a resource integrated with GlassFish Server through the connector adapter. We will discuss the integration with JMS resources in the next chapter.

Similar to JDBC connection pools and resources, Java EE defines the connector connection pools and resources. A connection pool is a group of reusable connections for a particular EIS. A connector resource is a program object that provides an application with a connection to an EIS.

The application locates the connector resource by looking up its JNDI name, just like working with a JDBC resource.

Creating a connector connection pool

To create a connector connection pool, we must first make sure that the connector module is deployed to the GlassFish Server. Similar to JDBC drivers, a connector module implements the mechanism by which a connection to the EIS system can be established. However, the deployment of a connector module is different than JDBC drivers. Instead of just copying the connector module archive to a directory, we need to use the Admin Console or the `deploy` command of the `asadmin` CLI to deploy a connector module as an application component.

Connector modules can also be embedded into a Java EE enterprise application. In this case, we can simply deploy the EAR archive of the application. An embedded connector module is available for the containing application only.

Once the connector module is deployed, we can create a connector connection pool as follows:

1. Log on to the Admin Console.
2. In the navigation panel, expand the **Resources** and **Connectors** node, and click **Connection Pools**.
3. Click **New** in the main content panel.

   The connector connection pool creation interface has two steps. The first step gathers the information about the name, resource adapter (connector module) name, and the connector type.

4. On the first **Create Connector Connection Pool** page, specify the following settings:
    ◦ In the **Name** field, enter a logical name for the pool.
    ◦ Specify this name when creating a connector resource.
    ◦ Select an entry from the **Resource Adapter** combobox.
    ◦ The combobox displays a list of deployed resource adapters (connector modules).
    ◦ Select a value from the **Connection Definition** combobox.
    ◦ The choices in the combobox depend on the resource adapter you selected. The **Connection Definition** attribute identifies a resource adapter's connection-definition element in the ra.xml file.

5. The second step gathers additional information about the connector connection pool. On the next **Create Connector Connection Pool** page, perform these tasks:
    ◦ In the **General Settings** section, verify that the values are correct.
    ◦ For the fields in the **Pool Settings** section, the default values can be retained.
    ◦ In the **Additional Properties** table, add any required properties.

6. Once we finish providing the information, click **Finish** to create the connection pool.

The `create-connector-connection-pool` command of the `asadmin` CLI can be used to create connector connection pools, for example:

```
# cd $AS_INSTALL/bin
# ./asadmin create-connector-connection-pool --raname jmsra
--connectiondefinition javax.jms.ConnectionFactory MyJCAPool
```

Connector connection pools have the same collection of advanced properties as JDBC connection pools. Just as in JDBC connection pools, these properties are used by GlassFish to improve the reliability and performance of using these resources.

After configuring a connector connection pool, use the `asadmin ping-connection-pool` command to test the health of the underlying connections. Notice that unlike JDBC connection pools, which can be tested from the Admin Console, connector connection pools can only be tested using the `asadmin` CLI.

Once the connector connection pools are created, we can create connector resources. The steps of creating a connector resource are almost identical to JDBC resources: all we need is to specify the JNDI name of the resource, and the underlying connection pool.

Configuring JavaMail resources

The JavaMail API provides a platform and protocol-independent framework to build mail and messaging applications. The JavaMail API allows applications to implement e-mail features easily. The GlassFish Server includes the JavaMail API along with JavaMail service providers that allow an application component to send e-mail notifications over the Internet and to read e-mail from IMAP and POP3 mail servers.

Configuring the mail session

In JavaMail, the component that provides a main server and protocol abstraction is a JavaMail session. Application components can get a reference to a mail session through standard JNDI lookup or dependency injection. As a result of this, when we configure a JavaMail session, we need to provide the specific configuration data based on the mail product and protocol.

JavaMail sessions can be configured using the Admin Console or `asadmin` CLI.

To create a JavaMail session using the Admin Console, complete the following steps:

1. Log on to the Admin Console.

2. Expand the **Resources** node, and click **JavaMail Sessions** in the navigation panel.

3. Click **New**. The user interface for creating a new custom resource is illustrated in the following screenshot. Enter the necessary information, and click **OK**.

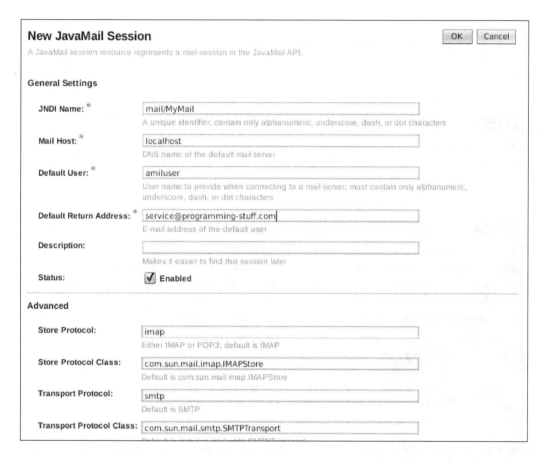

The Admin Console also allows us to update and delete Java Mail Sessions.

The `asadmin` CLI allows us to manage JavaMail Session resources from a command-line terminal. The command for adding a JavaMail session is `create-javamail-resource`, as demonstrated in the following example:

```
# cd $AS_INSTALL/bin
# ./asadmin create-javamail-resource -mailhost localhost -mailuser
MailUser -fromaddress service@programming-stuff.com  mail/MyMail
```

Similarly, the `delete-javamail-resources` and `list-javamail-resources` commands can be used to delete or list existing JavaMail resources.

 For a detailed explanation of each parameter we set while configuring JavaMail, refer to the GlassFish documentation.

Custom and external JNDI resources

Besides the standard resource types, GlassFish also supports two additional types of resources—custom and external. In this section, we examine their applicability, and discuss how to configure them.

Working with custom resources

A custom resource is typically a Java object that is read-only, and shared by many components in the application server runtime environment. A custom instance is always created by a factory object that implement the `javax.naming.spi.ObjectFactory` interface. When a custom resource is requested by an application component, the factory object will return the resource object.

 Because a custom resource is typically shared among all the application components, and it is typically read-only, its capability is rather limited. Therefore, it is mostly used to provide some additional configuration data for an environment, and it is not very suitable for hosting complicated application logic.

Custom resources are configured in the local naming service of GlassFish. A custom resource can be configured in two ways: Using the Admin Console, or using the `asadmin` CLI utility.

To create a custom resource using the Admin Console, complete the following steps:

1. Log on to the Admin Console.

2. Expand the **Resources** and **JNDI** nodes in the navigation panel. Click **Custom Resources**.

3. Click **New**. The user interface for creating a new custom resource is illustrated in the following screenshot. Enter the necessary information, and click **OK**.

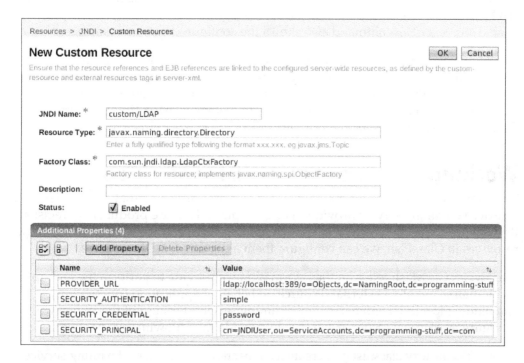

As we can see, depending on the type of the resource and its associated factory class, we may need to provide different properties to initiate the factory object. In our example, we attempt to configure a custom LDAP context resource so that applications can access the data stored in the corresponding LDAP server. In this case, we need to provide necessary properties, such as the URL and security credentials.

The Admin Console also allows us to update and delete custom resources.

The `asadmin` CLI allows us to manage custom resources from a command-line terminal. The command for adding a custom resource is `create-custom-resource`, as demonstrated in the following example:

```
# cd $AS_INSTALL
# ./asadmin create-custom-resource --restype com.programmingstuff.
jndi.CustomResource --factoryclass com.programmingstuff.jndi.
CustomResourceFactory custom/MyResource
```

Similarly, the `delete-custom-resources` and `list-custom-resources` commands can be used to delete or list existing custom resources. Furthermore, the output `list-jndi-entries` command also shows the configured custom resources.

Finally, we need to make sure that the custom resource's implementation classes (the resource and its corresponding factory class) are available for the application server domain. Typically, the custom resource's implementation should be archived into a JAR file and deployed to the `lib` directory of a domain. After the class library is deployed, we should restart the GlassFish Server to make it effective.

Working with external JNDI resources

Sometimes, Java EE applications need to access some resources that are registered in an external naming service provider. For example, a database product may register its database connection factory in its own naming service. If we want to utilize these resources in GlassFish, we can configure them as external JNDI resources.

Effectively, GlassFish relies on the information we provide to perform the lookup and initialization of an external resource on behalf of application components, and binds it to a JNDI name in its own naming service. Because of this, when we configure an external resource, we should provide the following information:

- The factory class used to create a connection to the external naming service
- The resource type
- Necessary properties

Not all the naming services can be used to configure external JNDI resources in GlassFish. The external JNDI factory class must implement `javax.naming.spi.InitialContextFactory` interface.

External resources are configured in the local naming service of GlassFish. An external resource can be configured in two ways: using the Admin Console or using the `asadmin` CLI utility.

To create an external resource using the Admin Console, complete the following steps:

1. Log on to the Admin Console.

2. Expand the **Resources** and **JNDI** nodes in the navigation panel. Click **External Resources**.

3. Click **New**. The user interface for creating a new external resource is illustrated in the following screenshot. Enter the necessary information, and click **OK**.

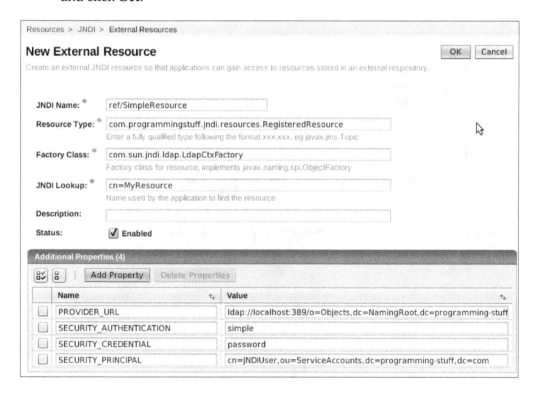

As we can see, depending on the type of the external naming service, we need to specify the appropriate resource type, factory type, and necessary properties. In our example, we attempt to configure an external JNDI resource that is stored in an LDAP server. In this case, we need to provide necessary properties, such as provider URL and security credentials for the LDAP connection factory class.

The Admin Console also allows us to update and delete external resources.

The `asadmin` CLI allows us to manage custom resources from a command-line terminal. The command for adding a custom resource is `create-jndi-resource`, as demonstrated in the following example:

```
# cd $AS_INSTALL/bin
# ./asadmin create-jndi-resource --lookupname cn=MyResources --restype
com.programmingstuff.jndi.RegistryResource --factoryclass com.sun.jndi.
ldap.LdapCtxFactory ref/SimpleResource
```

Similarly, the `delete-jndi-resources` and `list-jndi-resources` commands can be used to delete or list existing external resources.

Finally, we need to make sure that the external resource's implementation classes (the resource and its corresponding factory class) are available for the application server domain. Typically, the custom resource's implementation should be archived into a JAR file and deployed to the `lib` directory of a domain. After the class library is deployed, we should bounce the GlassFish Server to make it effective.

Summary

This chapter provided you with an introduction to resource management and deployment in GlassFish. At this point, you should have a good understanding of the resource types supported by GlassFish, and how to configure them. In the next chapter, we will discuss how to configure a special type of resource—JMS resources.

6

Configuring JMS Resources

In this chapter, we will discuss how to configure **Java Message Service (JMS)** resources in GlassFish. We will begin the chapter with an overview of message systems and the support of JMS on GlassFish. We will then discuss how to configure two popular open source JMS service providers, the **Open Message Queue (Open MQ)** and Apache ActiveMQ.

JMS support on GlassFish

Message-based solutions are playing an increasingly important role nowadays, as more and more systems need to be integrated together and need to communicate with each other in a loosely-coupled manner. In this section, we briefly introduce the core concepts of messaging system and the JMS standard, and then describe how GlassFish supports JMS resources.

Message-based systems and JMS

A simplified view of a typical message-based system is illustrated in the following figure.

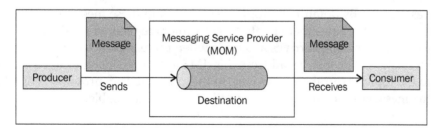

As shown in the figure, the communication pattern of a messaging-based system is different from the client-server paradigm, where application components communicate with each other directly. Instead, in a message-based system, the communication among application components (producers and consumers) is mediated by a message service provider. As a result of this, a message service provider is sometimes referred to as a **Message Oriented Middleware** (**MOM**). The producer creates a message that contains relevant data, and sends it to a destination resource maintained by the message service provider. The message is then routed to consumer components that are registered to the specific destination.

Another distinct feature of a message-based system is that the message service provider effectively makes the communication between producers and consumers asynchronous. When a producer sends a message, consumers do not need to be available because the message service provider can persist the message until the consumer becomes available. In fact, the producer and consumer do not need to have any knowledge of each other, as long as the message is in a format that is agreed upon. This feature further decouples the producers and consumers.

JMS defines a standard Java API for application components to create, send, receive, and process messages. It also provides a standard API that simplifies how application components interact with a JMS-compliant message service provider (JMS provider for short). It defines the connection factory and destinations of the JMS provider in the form of administered objects, which can be registered in a JNDI naming service. An application component can use the standard JNDI API to perform a lookup operation to retrieve these resources. This approach reduces the vendor-dependency when we build a JMS application.

JMS defines the two messaging approaches as follows:

- **Point-to-Point** (**PTP**): A producer sends messages to a *queue* destination, which retains the messages until they are successfully routed to a consumer. Furthermore, each message is received by only one consumer.

- **Publish/Subscribe** (**Pub/Sub**): A producer sends messages to a *topic* destination. By default, the topic does not retain these messages. Instead, it immediately routes them to all the consumers registered for the topic. Due to this, if a message arrives at a topic when there is no active consumer, the message will be lost. To address this, JMS allows a consumer to be registered to the topic as durable subscriber. In this case, the JMS provider will retain the messages for this consumer until it becomes available.

The JMS API became an integral part of the Java EE since version 1.3 as the standard to integrate with messaging systems. Subsequent Java EE revisions further enhanced the JMS API and messaging system integration in the following areas:

- **Message-Driven Beans (MDB)**: An MDB is a container-managed component that can asynchronously consume messages sent to a JMS destination. Due to this, we can consider an MDB as an asynchronous message listener component. The application server's MDB container provides services for MDBs such as life cycle management, instance pooling and naming services. These services eliminate a lot of boiler-plate code necessary to create a message listener object. Due to this, when implementing an MDB, the developer only needs to focus on the logic about how to process messages delivered to the MDB. Furthermore, the MDB container's instance pooling service can significantly improve the throughput of processing messages routed to a specific MDB.

- **Java Connector Architecture (JCA)**: Through JCA resource adapters, JMS providers can be easily integrated into different application servers. Once integrated, application components can treat them as standard JCA resources, and interact with the resources in a provider-independent manner.

GlassFish support for JMS

The GlassFish Server contains a built-in JMS service provider, the Open MQ (https://mq.dev.java.net). It also includes a generic JCA resource adapter that can be used to integrate with most JMS providers. GlassFish also provides a configurable MDB container implementation to host message driven beans. In this chapter, we discuss how GlassFish integrates with two different JMS providers—the Open MQ and Apache ActiveMQ (http://activemq.apache.org). We also discuss how we can configure the MDB container and MDB components to work with a JMS service provider.

One of the most commonly asked questions is "Which JMS provider is better, or at least which open source JMS provider is better?". The answer to this question typically depends heavily on the experience of the individual or organization. Most reputable JMS implementations, including Open MQ and ActiveMQ are capable of processing large volumes of messages efficiently.

Between Open MQ and ActiveMQ, my personal favorite choice is the former. The reason is not because Open MQ is bundled in GlassFish. It is actually because my experience with the Open MQ product dates back to the days of its commercial ancestor, the Sun ONE Message Queue. I have always appreciated its straightforward administration interface and thorough documentation. Furthermore, I have successfully created many production deployments by using the product. Make no mistake though; I have also witnessed organizations using ActiveMQ successfully in production. Also, ActiveMQ is under active development, and it is bundled in several very good open source products as the default JMS provider.

Now, let's discuss how GlassFish works with the Open MQ product (https://mq.dev.java.net).

Getting started with Open MQ

An evolution of the Sun Java System Message Queue (formerly Sun ONE Message Queue), Open MQ is a very active open source sub-project of GlassFish. Open MQ implements a high-performance JMS provider. In addition to its high performance, and being fully JMS compliant, Open MQ provides many other features, such as message broker cluster support, SOAP/HTTP message support, C/C++ Client API support, and so on. Due to this, some people said Open MQ was the best kept secret within the Sun middleware software stack.

The GlassFish Server is shipped with the Open MQ product. In addition, the GlassFish administration infrastructure provides some basic capabilities for configuring the Open MQ.

The open source distribution of the GlassFish server you download from the GlassFish project site includes the "community edition" of Open MQ. This edition does not include some of the additional features such as C-API support. If you need to use these features, you can either download or install the Sun supported GlassFish Enterprise Server distribution, or download and install a full version of the Open MQ product. We should expect that in future versions of GlassFish, the bundled Open MQ will be a feature-complete distribution.

By default, the bundled Open MQ is configured to have a small footprint without many advanced features. In this section, we will first get familiar with the Open MQ product, and later in this chapter we will show you how to configure the Open MQ to work with GlassFish and Java EE application components.

First, let's examine the high-level architecture of GlassFish, and learn the meaning of some critical concepts along the way.

The architecture of Open MQ

The high-level architecture of Open MQ is illustrated in the following figure.

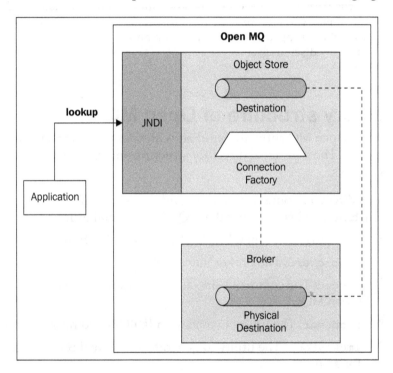

The main components illustrated in this figure are explained as follows:

- The **Broker** can be considered as a complete instance of the message provider. A broker contains physical destinations (both queues and topics), and it is responsible for routing messages sent from producers to the appropriate destination, and delivering messages from destinations to registered consumers. The broker supports multiple connection mechanisms between application components and the broker, and it can also be configured with different performance and security features.

- In order to simplify and standardize the JMS programming model, JMS defines two types of administered objects—connection factories and destinations. A **Connection Factory** is an object that encapsulates all the vendor-specific information necessary for a client to establish a connection to the broker, and the destination object provides a logical reference to a physical destination. These two administered objects are registered in a JNDI-compliant object store, and a client can perform a standard JNDI lookup to retrieve these objects. Once these objects are retrieved, the client can produce and consume messages.

A client can create these objects programmatically. For example, a client may want to use some vendor-specific features or APIs that cannot be encapsulated in a standard manner. However, this practice is highly discouraged.

The directory structure of Open MQ

The binary of the Open MQ software bundled with GlassFish is installed at `$AS_INSTALL/imq`. The high-level directory structure and essential files are described as follows:

- The `bin` directory contains the command line and GUI utilities for administering and controlling the MQ. The essential utilities include:

    ○ `imqadmin`: The Open MQ GUI-based administration console.

    ○ `imqbrokerd`: The broker management utility.

    ○ `imqcmd`: The command-line administration utility of Open MQ.

    ○ `imqdbmgr`: The utility to manage a JDBC-based message store.

    ○ `imqkeytool`: The utility to generate self-signed SSL certificate for a broker.

    ○ `imqobjmgr`: The utility to manage administered objects, including connection factory and destinations.

    ○ `imqusermgr`: The utility to manage the flat file user repository for the Open MQ.

- The `demo` directory contains a variety of demo applications for Open MQ.

- The `etc` directory contains the Open MQ server-wide configuration file— `imqenv.conf`. This file effectively defines the environment variables for the Open MQ installation. For example, you should find the following line near the end of the file:

  `IMQ_DEFAULT_VARHOME=/opt/glassfish/domains/domain1/imq`

  This line specifies that by default, all the brokers created within this Open MQ installation will be inside the `/opt/glassfish/domains/domain1/imq` directory.

- The `include` directory contains the C API header files for building C-based clients.

- The `javadoc` contains the Java API documentation for Open MQ.

- The `lib` directory contains the Java and C libraries for the Open MQ.

- The `var` directory is empty. In a standalone installation, this directory is the default root directory for all the brokers created.

Once GlassFish is installed, a default OpenMQ broker, `imqbroker` is also created within the default domain in `$AS_INSTALL/domains/domain1/imq/instances/imqbroker`. The main content of this directory includes:

- The `etc` directory contains two files, the `passwd` is a password file for users configured for the broker, and the `accesscontrol.properties` file allows us to specify different types of access controls for different users.

- The `fs370` directory is the flat file-based persistence store for messages and transactions.

- The `log` directory contains the rotated log files of running the broker.

- The `props` directory contains the `config.properties` file, which describes most of the properties configured for the broker.

In the following section, we show you how to configure Open MQ.

Configuring Open MQ

There are two ways to configure and administer the Open MQ server product:

- The first option is to use the JMS configuration capability built into the GlassFish's administrative infrastructure, such as Admin Console and the `asadmin` CLI utility. This option has the advantage of being simple, because we use the familiar GlassFish administration interfaces. The drawback of this option, however, is that the capability is limited. For example, we cannot create a multi-broker cluster.

- The second option relies on the tools provided in the Open MQ binary discussed in the previous section, such as `imqbrokerd` and `imqadmin`. This option has the advantage of having full control of the Open MQ. The drawback of this approach is that we need to use a completely different set of tools, rather than the GlassFish Server.

In the following sections, we discuss the essential configuration tasks for Open MQ:

- Configuring the Open MQ runtime environment
- Configuring the physical destinations within Open MQ
- Configuring administrative objects, including connection factories and destination

First, let's look at how to configure Open MQ using the GlassFish administration interfaces

Configuring Open MQ within GlassFish

By default, when we start the GlassFish Server, the server process starts the Open MQ's default broker using a separate thread. Once successfully started, the broker listens on the default port 7676 for client connection requests.

Configuring the Open MQ Runtime

To configure the Open MQ Runtime environment, complete the following steps:

1. Log on to the Admin Console.

2. In the navigation panel, expand the **Configuration** node, and click the **Java Message Service** node, as shown in the following image.

The Admin Console displays the properties of the JMS Service configured with Open MQ as the JMS provider. Using the Admin Console, we can configure many properties that determine how GlassFish maintains the connection with the Open MQ broker. For example, whether GlassFish will attempt to reconnect to the Open MQ broker if a connection is lost, and the frequency with which reconnection attempts are carried out. The Admin Console Help document provides detailed definitions for these properties.

These properties can also be managed using the `get` or `set` commands of the `asadmin` CLI utility. For example, to check if reconnection attempts are allowed, we can use the following command:

```
# cd $AS_INSTALL/bin
# ./asadmin get server.jms-service.reconnect-enabled
```

Also, as we can see in this diagram, the default runtime type of Open MQ is **EMBEDDED**. The embedded execution type runs both the GlassFish Server and the Open MQ in the same process, thus, it has a very small memory footprint. However, it is not very reliable, because both GlassFish and Open MQ run in the same JVM. If one of them has issues, such as a memory leak, then the other server will also be affected.

The other two runtime types are **LOCAL** and **REMOTE**. In the **LOCAL** runtime type, GlassFish and Open MQ run in two separate JVM processes. When we use the `asadmin` CLI to start/stop the GlassFish Server, the Open MQ process is also started/stopped. The **LOCAL** runtime mode is more reliable because the server processes are independent of each other.

Under the **REMOTE** runtime type, the GlassFish Server does not control the life cycle of the Open MQ server. Instead, GlassFish will communicate with the Open MQ broker instance running on the host identified by the `Default_JMS_Host` property, as shown in the screenshot. Notice that value of the `Default_JMS_Host` property must be predefined as a valid JMS host. This can be done by clicking the **JMS Hosts** node in the navigation panel, and adding new JMS host values.

Notice that when we switch the runtime nodes, we need to restart GlassFish to make sure that the change is persistent.

Under the **EMBEDDED** and **LOCAL** types, we can use the GlassFish Admin Console to create and delete physical JMS destinations in the Open MQ broker instance. To do this, click the **Physical Destinations** node in the navigation panel. The main content panel lists the existing destinations, and it also provides the options for creating and deleting physical destinations. Physical destinations can also be created using the `create-jmsdest` command of the `asadmin` CLI utility.

Now that we have Open MQ runtime configured, in the next section, let's discuss how to configure JMS resources in GlassFish so that they can be used by our applications, such as message-driven beans and clients that produce messages.

Configuring the JMS Resources

To configure JMS Resources, complete the following steps:

1. Log on to the Admin Console.

2. In the navigation panel, expand the **Resources** node, and then expand the **JMS Resources** node.

The Admin Console displays the JMS resources, as shown in the following screenshot.

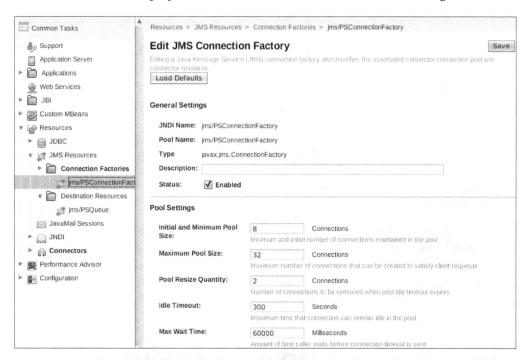

As we can see, the two types of JMS resources we can configure are **JMS Connection Factories**, and **Destination Resources**.

To create a connection factory, click the **Connection Factories** node in the navigation panel, and click **New** in the main content panel. In the new connection factory form, we need to specify the following information:

- The JNDI name of the connection factory, which typically starts with a prefix jms, such as jms/MyCF.

- The type of the connection factory, which should be javax.jms. ConnectionFactory for JMS 1.1 compliant JMS providers and clients, as it provides a unified interface for both queue and topic connection factories.

- Necessary additional properties. If we are using the Open MQ running in the **EMBEDDED** or **LOCAL** mode, then we don't need to provide any additional information. If we are using a remote JMS broker, then we should add a new property — `AddressList` — and set the value to a comma-separated list of `host:port` combinations. This list describes the locations where the Open MQ broker or broker cluster is running.

To create a destination resource, in the Admin Console, click the **Destination Resources** node in the navigation panel, and click **New** in the main content panel. In the new destination resource form, we need to specify the following information:

- The JNDI name of the destination, which typically starts with a prefix `jms`, such as `jms/MyQueue`.

- The name of the **Physical Destination** applied to the destination resource.

- The type of the connection factory, which could be `javax.jms.Queue` or `javax.jms.Topic`.

Once the JMS resources are created, we can create and deploy applications to take advantage of these resources. In the `example` directory, a very simple MDB and a JMS application client are provided. Please refer to the example `README` file for more information.

As discussed earlier in the Open MQ architecture, physical destinations are maintained by the Open MQ broker instance, not by GlassFish. Due to this, the GlassFish Admin Console does not provide options to configure properties of the physical destination, such as durable subscriptions for topics. In order to configure these properties, we have to use the Open MQ's standalone tools, which will be presented later in this chapter.

Configuring Open MQ using standalone tools

Open MQ is shipped with a collection of utilities that can be used to configure and administer its runtime environment and resources. In this section, we provide a brief introduction to these utilities. For a detailed description of these utilities, you can refer to the Open MQ document set, located at `http://docs.sun.com/app/docs/coll/1307.6`.

Starting and stopping the Open MQ broker

The imqbrokerd utility is used to start a message broker. To start the default broker configured for GlassFish, open a command-line terminal, and enter the following commands:

```
# cd $AS_INSTALL/imq/bin
# ./imqbrokerd -tty
```

You should see an output describing the information about the broker, and the confirmation of the successful start of the broker.

If we do not specify a broker name, the imqbrokerd command will try to start the default broker named imqbroker. We can also supply a name <broker_name>. If the broker named <broker_name> is already created, then the imqbrokerd command starts it; otherwise, a new broker of this name is created and then started.

To shutdown the message broker, enter *Ctrl+C* in the terminal where imqbrokerd is running.

 Refer to the Open MQ documentation for information on how to run Open MQ brokers as a service.

Administering the Open MQ Broker using imqcmd

The main CLI utility we use to manage the Open MQ is imqcmd. It supports a long list of commands that can be used to create, destroy, modify, and display the information of a resource, such as a broker or a physical destination, and so on. To show the commands and options supported, enter the following commands in a terminal:

```
# cd $AS_INSTALL/imq/bin
# ./imqcmd -h
```

As the first example, we can use the following command to display the status information of the currently running broker:

```
# cd $AS_INSTALL/imq/bin
# ./imqcmd query bkr -u admin
```

Once you are prompted to enter the password, enter the default password admin. You should see an output describing the information regarding the currently running broker.

We can store the password in a password file and use the `-passfile` option to point to this file.

As another example, the following command queries the physical queue destination named `PSQueueDest`, and displays its information in the command-line terminal.

```
# cd $AS_INSTALL/imq/bin
# ./imqcmd query dst -t q -n PSQueueDest -u admin
```

In this example, the option `-t` specifies the type of the destination as a topic, and the option `-n PSQueueDest` specifies the name of the physical destination.

Refer to the help information and the MQ Administration Guide for a detailed description of the `imqcmd` utility.

Using the imqadmin administration console

The `imqadmin` utility is the primary GUI-based administration console of the Open MQ. It supports more of the functions of the `imqcmd` utility. Besides, it can also manage and configure the administration objects used by applications, such as specifying a naming service provider, and registering connection factories and destination resources in the naming service.

To start the administration console, open a command-line terminal, and type the following command:

```
# cd $AS_INSTALL/imq/bin
# ./imqadmin
```

You should see the administrator console window displayed. The administration console's navigation pane contains two top-level nodes, **Brokers** and **Object Stores**. The **Brokers** node organizes all the registered Open MQ brokers being managed by the administration console. The **Object Stores** node organizes the naming service providers to which the JMS administration objects (connection factories and destination resources) are registered.

The following steps walk you through the typical process of adding a broker, and managing the broker resources.

1. From the navigation pane of the administrator console, right click the **Brokers** node, and choose **Add Broker**. You should see a dialog box displayed.

2. Fill out the **Add Broker** dialog according to the following screenshot, enter **admin** in the password field, and click **OK**.

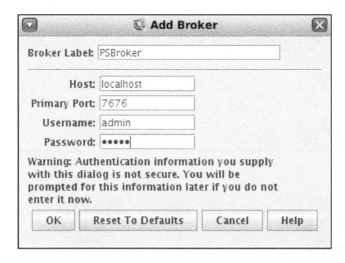

Now you should see the broker **PSBroker** is listed under the **Brokers** node with a red **X** on its icon, which indicates that the broker is not currently connected to the administrator console yet.

Adding a broker does not create or start a new physical broker. It merely registers an existing broker to the administration console, and once we connect the administration console, we will be able to manage the resources of the broker.

3. From the navigation pane, right click **PSBroker** under the **Brokers** node, and choose **Connect to Broker**. Once you connect to the broker, you should see the red **X** disappeared on the **Brokers** node.

4. From the navigation pane, click **Services** under **PSBroker**. In the result pane, you should see all the available connection services listed for the broker, as shown in the following screenshot.

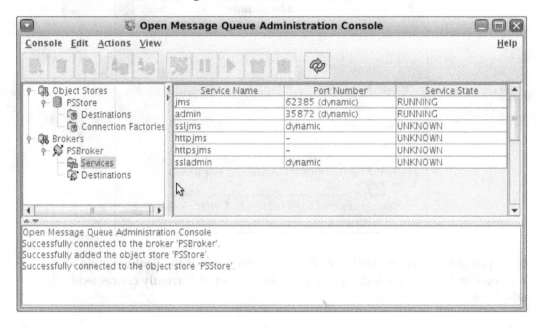

5. From the navigation pane, right click **Destinations** under **PSBroker**, and select **Add Broker Destination**. You should see a dialog displayed.

6. Enter **PSQueueDest** in the **Destination Name** field, select **Queue** radio button if not already selected. Keep all the other settings unchanged, and click **OK** to add the physical destination.

7. From the navigation pane, click **Destinations** under **PSBroker**, the newly added **PSQueueDest** should appear.

With physical destinations created, we can go through the following steps to configure the connection factory and destination resources in the **Object Stores**:

1. Right click the **Object Stores** node in the navigation pane, and choose **Add Object Store**.

2. Enter the following information in the dialog, and click **OK** to add the **Object Store**.

   ° Enter **PSStore** in the **Object Store Label** field.

   ° From the **Name** pull-down menu, select java.naming. factory.initial, and enter com.sun.jndi.fscontext. RefFSContextFactory in the value field.

○ Click the **Add** button. These steps set the JNDI service provider you will use, to a filesystem based object store.

○ From the **Name** pull-down menu, select `java.naming.provider.url`, and enter `file:///tmp` in the value field. Click the **Add** button. These steps set the exact location of the object store to the directory `/tmp`.

In the navigation pane, you will see the object store **PSStore** you just added is listed under the **Object Stores** node with a red **X** on its icon, which indicates that the object store is not currently connected to the administrator console yet.

3. From the navigation pane, right click **PSStore** under the **Object Stores** node, and choose **Connect to Object Store**. Once you connect to the object store, you should see that the red **X** has disappeared on the **Object Stores** node.

4. From the navigation pane of the Open MQ administrator console, right click **Destinations** under **PSStore** node, and select **Add Destination Object**. You should see a dialog box displayed.

5. Enter **PSQueue** in the **Lookup Name** field, select **Queue** from the **Destination Type** radio button. Enter **PSQueueDest** in the **Destination Name** field, and click **OK** to add the queue destination, as shown in the following screenshot.

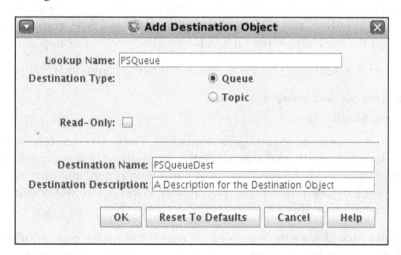

Now that we have seen how Open MQ is integrated with GlassFish, let's look at another very popular open source JMS implementation, ActiveMQ.

Configuring ActiveMQ for GlassFish

ActiveMQ is a very popular open source provider that is fully JMS 1.1 compliant. Besides, Active MQ has several very appealing features, such as cross language support for client development, high availability support, and support for REST API, and so on. For a more detailed description of the ActiveMQ product, visit the ActiveMQ project website hosted by Apache: `http://activemq.apache.org`.

GlassFish is shipped with a generic JMS JCA resource adapter. In this section, we use ActiveMQ as an example to demonstrate how this generic resource adapter allows GlassFish to integrate with third-party JMS providers.

> Many JMS providers, including ActiveMQ includes its own JCA resource adapters for integrating with a Java EE application server. In this book, we do not cover this topic. You can refer to the JMS provider's documentation to enable this. For example, integrating ActiveMQ into GlassFish using ActiveMQ's resource adapter is actually quite similar to using the GlassFish resource adapter.

Installing and configuring ActiveMQ

The first step of integrating with ActiveMQ is to install it. Installing ActiveMQ is very straight forward. Simply download the latest ActiveMQ binary distribution (ZIP format for Window, and GZIP for UNIX/Linux/Mac OS X) from `http://activemq.apache.org`, and extract it to a target directory. For example, `/opt`.

Next, let's start the ActiveMQ broker with the following commands:

```
# cd  /opt/apache-activemq-5.3.0/bin
# ./activemq-admin start
```

There are a variety of ways to configure ActiveMQ. The most comprehensive mechanism is to work with XML-based configuration files. This approach can be used to define all aspects of a message broker and its components, such as message destination. For a detailed discussion, please refer to the ActiveMQ documentation for more information on this.

ActiveMQ also provides a simple web-based user interface for basic administrative tasks, such as creating/deleting message destinations (both topics and queues), sending messages to a destination for testing, and browsing messages in a destination, and so on.

Now let's use the administrative user interface to configure a queue. To do this, complete the following steps:

- Open a browser, and access the ActiveMQ admin URL `http://localhost:8161/admin`. The ActiveMQ administration page appears.

- Click **Queues**.

The browser lists the message queues configured for the ActiveMQ broker. By default, a queue named **example.A** is configured, as shown in the following screenshot.

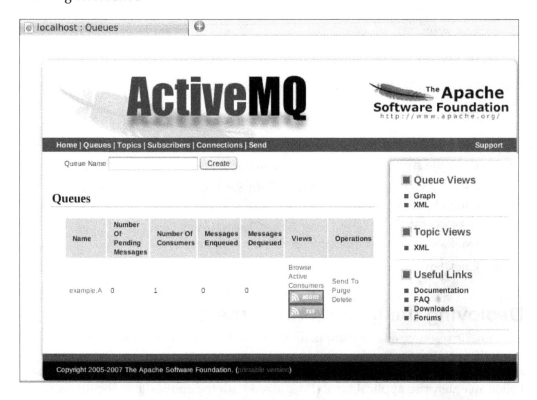

In the next section, we show you how to integrate this sample queue into GlassFish.

Working with GlassFish generic resource adapter

In this section, we show you the necessary configuration steps in GlassFish to integrate with ActiveMQ.

Configuring the GlassFish server classpath

In order to integrate with ActiveMQ, we need to add the following files to the GlassFish server classpath:

`$ACTIVEMQ_HOME/lib/commons-logging-1.1.jar`

`$ACTIVEMQ_HOME/lib/activemq-core-5.3.0.jar`

`$ACTIVEMQ_HOME/lib/optional/activeio-core-3.1.2.jar`

To add these files to the GlassFish classpath, complete the following steps:

1. Log on to the GlassFish Admin Console.
2. Click the **Application Server** node in the navigation panel.
3. Click **JVM Settings** tab, and then **Path Settings** tab in the main content panel.
4. Add the full paths of the files to the **Classpath Suffix** field. (Make sure you use the appropriate file separator).
5. Click **Save**, and then restart GlassFish.

Deploying the generic resource adapter

The generic resource adapter shipped with GlassFish is located at `$AS_INSTALL/ lib/addons/resourceadapters/genericjmsra/genericra.rar`. Like all resource adapters, it can be deployed as a standalone connector module, or it can be bundled inside an enterprise application and deployed with the application. The difference is that if it is deployed along as part of an application, it will only be visible to that application. In this chapter, we deploy the resource adapter as a standalone connector module.

To do this, first, we need to create a `resource-adapter-config` object in the GlassFish domain configuration. This is one of the few tasks that can only be executed using the `asadmin` CLI utility, as shown in the following command:

```
# cd $AS_INSTALL/bin
# asadmin create-resource-adapter-config --property SupportsXA=true:RMPo
licy=OnePerPhysicalConnection:ProviderIntegrationMode=javabean:Connection
FactoryClassName=org.apache.activemq.ActiveMQConnectionFactory:QueueConn
ectionFactoryClassName=org.apache.activemq.ActiveMQConnectionFactory:Topi
cConnectionFactoryClassName=org.apache.activemq.ActiveMQConnectionFactory
:XAConnectionFactoryClassName=org.apache.activemq.ActiveMQXAConnectionFa
ctory:XAQueueConnectionFactoryClassName=org.apache.activemq.ActiveMQXACo
nnectionFactory:XATopicConnectionFactoryClassName=org.apache.activemq.Act
iveMQXAConnectionFactory:UnifiedDestinationClassName=org.apache.activemq.
command.ActiveMQDestination:QueueClassName=org.apache.activemq.command.Ac
tiveMQQueue:TopicClassName=org.apache.activemq.command.ActiveMQTopic:Conn
ectionFactoryProperties=brokerURL\\=tcp\\://127.0.0.1\\:61616:LogLevel=FI
NE genericra
```

Make sure the second command is entered in one single line. Essentially, this command specifies the connection factory classes the Generic Resource Adapter will use to interact with ActiveMQ, and it also specifies some essential properties that contain the information about the ActiveMQ provider. For example, the `ConnectionFactoryProperties` property's value, URL=`tcp://127.0.0.1:61616` specifies the listening port of the ActiveMQ broker.

> The \\ in the command is to escape the = sign in the property value. If you are running the command on Windows platform, you only need to use a single \. Also, for ActiveMQ, make sure we specify the property `supportsXA=true` in the command. Otherwise, the generic resource adapter won't work.

After creating the resource adapter configuration, we can deploy the resource adapter using the following command:

```
# cd $AS_INSTALL/bin
# ./asadmin deploy ../lib/addons/resourceadapters/genericjmsra/genericra.
rar
```

We can also deploy the resource adapter as a connector module using the Admin Console. The command-line based deployment is found to be faster.

Creating the connector resources

After deploying the resource adapter, we can now create necessary connector resources to enable the integration with ActiveMQ. These resources can be created using the Admin Console or the `asadmin` CLI. This section shows you how to do it using the CLI. In the Admin Console, these tasks are grouped under the **Connectors** node under **Resources**.

First, we need to create a connector connection pool:

```
# cd $AS_INSTALL/bin

# ./asadmin create-connector-connection-pool --raname genericra
--connectiondefinition javax.jms.QueueConnectionFactory
--transactionsupport XATransaction AMGConnectionFactoryPool
```

Next, we can create a connector connection factory using the `AMGConnectionFactoryPool` we just created:

```
# cd $AS_INSTALL/bin

# ./asadmin create-connector-resource --poolname AMGConnectionFactoryPool
jms/AMGConnectionFactoryPool
```

Finally, we can create a connector administration object as follows:

```
# cd $AS_INSTALL/bin

# ./asadmin create-admin-object --raname genericra --restype javax.
jms.Queue --property DestinationProperties=PhysicalName=example.A jms/
AMGQueue
```

After these steps, sample queue, `example.A` in the ActiveMQ installation becomes an accessible JMS resource. For example, we can develop an MDB to listen to all the messages sent to this queue. For more information, you can refer to the sample applications for this chapter.

Summary

This chapter provides you with an introduction to configuring JMS resources in GlassFish. At this point, you should be familiar with the Open MQ component that is built into GlassFish, and you should understand how to use the provided JCA resource adapter to integrate other JMS service providers with GlassFish. This chapter also shows you how to configure the MDB container, which allows us to configure the runtime environment for message-driven beans.

In the next chapter, we will discuss another important aspect of GlassFish, security.

7
Securing GlassFish

In this chapter, we will discuss the security aspect of the GlassFish Server. We will begin the chapter with a quick review of some concepts essential for understanding the Java EE security model. We will then introduce the security features supported by the GlassFish Server. Finally, we will show you how we can secure both the GlassFish Server and the applications deployed to it. The goal of this chapter is to help you get familiar with the utilities used to establish a secure runtime environment for GlassFish.

Reviewing essential security concepts

In this section, let's first consider some common security concerns, and some important concepts associated with them. These concepts are essential for understanding the security model implemented in GlassFish.

Authentication

Authentication refers to the mechanism by which communicating entities (users, servers, or application components) prove to one another that they are who they claim they are.

Authentication is typically based on authentication realms, or realms for short. A realm typically contains many users (also known as security principals) and their security credentials. Users contained in a realm can be authenticated based on their credentials, such as the username and password. Users defined in a realm may be assigned to groups. Examples of authentication realms include **Lightweight Directory Access Protocol (LDAP)** servers and relational database tables.

Authorization

Authorization refers to the mechanism to restrict access to applications and resources based on certain security attributes associated with authenticated entities.

Common mechanisms of authorizing resource access include **Access Control Lists (ACL)** and role-based access control (RBAC). The Java EE security model defines a role-based authorization mechanism, where the access privileges for certain resources (such as URLs within a web application) are associated with application-specific roles. Java EE defines a standard mechanism to map users and groups in a physical realm to logical roles defined in an application. The mapping can be based on user's identity or group membership. This mapping is illustrated in the following figure:

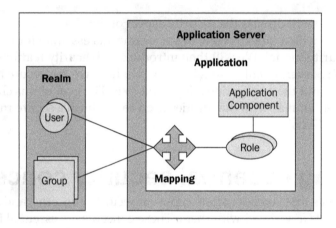

Within a secure Java EE application, the access control is defined based on roles, which can be either declared in the `role-name` element of the deployment descriptor, such as `web.xml`, or declared using the `@DeclareRoles` annotation in the application component. The application server-specific deployment descriptor, such as `sun-web.xml` for GlassFish provides the mapping between users/groups in a realm and roles defined in the application. In other words, once a user is authenticated successfully, whether he or she is allowed to access a resource depends fully on whether the roles to which the user is mapped have the permission.

Data integrity and confidentiality

Data integrity refers to the mechanism to ensure that data communicated between two entities is not altered by an unauthorized third party. Data integrity verification can be implemented with message digest algorithm, where the data is transmitted along with a short digest calculated from the original data. Upon receiving the data, the recipient calculates the digest with the same algorithm, and compares the calculated digest with the received.

Confidentiality refers to the mechanism used to ensure that information is made available only to the intended entity that is authorized to access it. Confidentiality of communication is achieved by encrypting the data transmitted.

In practice, the data integrity and confidentiality are typically addressed at the communication protocol level using **Secure Socket Layer (SSL)**, its successor, **Transport Level Security (TLS)**, and HTTPS.

Auditing

Auditing refers to the mechanism to maintain the record of security-related events so that the overall effectiveness of the security solution can be assessed. Auditing is typically implemented with logging mechanism, where each security-related activity that has occurred in the system is persistently recorded.

Understanding security features in GlassFish

Besides being fully compliant with the Java EE security model, the GlassFish Server also supports several additional capabilities. Overall, the GlassFish Server's security features include the following:

- Full compliance with the Java EE security model.
- Supports multiple authentication realms, and supports customized realm.
- Supports both declarative and programmatic security configuration.
- Supports **Java Authorization Contract for Containers (JACC)** pluggable authorization (JSR-155).
- Supports message-level security for web service components.
- Supports single sign-on across all GlassFish Server applications within a single security domain.
- Supports Programmatic logins.

In the following sections, we will discuss the security features of the GlassFish Server, and we will also introduce necessary utilities and tools which can be used to configure these security features. First, let's see how we can manage user authentication in GlassFish.

Configuring user authentication

User authentication in GlassFish is managed in realms. GlassFish is shipped with three pre-configured realms, and it also includes several additional realm implementations we can use to create realms based on common user repositories such as LDAP servers and database tables. We can use the Admin Console to create new realms and view or delete existing realms. To do this, simply expand the **Configuration** node in the navigation panel, then expand the **Security** node, and click **Realms**. The following screenshot shows the Admin Console user interface for managing realms.

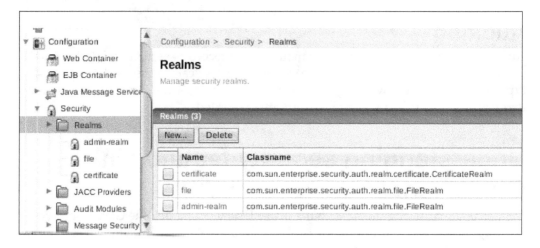

Also, the following commands of the asadmin CLI utility allow us to manage authentication realms:

- **create-auth-realm**
- **list-auth-realms**
- **delete-auth-realm**

For example, the list-auth-realms command displays the realms configured for a running GlassFish Server.

Next, we explain how to configure the authentication realms supported in GlassFish.

GlassFish also supports customized authentication realms. The implementation of such a realm is beyond the scope of this book. You can refer to the GlassFish Server Developer Guide (http://docs.sun.com/app/docs/doc/820-4336) for more information.

Security realms supported in GlassFish

Out of box, GlassFish is configured with three authentication realms — two file-based realms, and a certificate-based realm. Furthermore, GlassFish is also shipped with several other realm implementations. In this section, let's examine each type of the realm supported by GlassFish.

The file realm

The default realm name is file. If an application does not explicitly specify an authentication realm, then the file realm is used. The file realm stores username, password, and groups in keyfile, a text file located at $AS_INSTALL/domains/domain1/config. The entries of this file have the following format:

```
user;{SSHA}z0fakmQryoMzuirbekDdhGn5FW9MIYkixqG5dg==;g1,g2
```

The semicolons (;) in these entries separate the following parts sequentially — the username, the encrypted password, and a comma-separated list of groups to which the user belongs.

Another realm, admin-realm is also a file realm that stores user credentials in the file admin-keyfile, located at $AS_INSTALL/domains/domain1/config. The admin-realm is the default realm that stores the credentials of the GlassFish Server administrators.

For flat file-based realms such as file and admin-realm, we can use both Admin Console and asadmin CLI utilities to manage them. To use the Admin Console, click on the target realm, such as **file**, and then click the **Manage User** button.

The following commands of the asadmin CLI utilities can be used to manage user entries in file-based realms:

- list-file-groups
- list-file-users
- create-file-user
- update-file-user
- delete-file-user

For example, the following command lists the users in the `file` realm:

```
# cd #AS_INSTALL/bin
# ./asadmin list-file-users
```

The `--authrealmname` option of these commands can be used to specify the target file-based realm we are working with. For example, the following commands list the users in the `admin-realm`:

```
# cd $AS_INSTALL/bin
# ./asadmin list-file-users --authrealmname=admin-realm
```

The certificate realm

Another preconfigured realm in GlassFish is called `certificate`. With the `certificate` realm, GlassFish authenticates users based on their client certificates. In order to authenticate user's client certificate, GlassFish must be able to trust the **Certificate Authority (CA)** who issued these certificates. This is done by including trusted CA's certificates or public keys in a trusted key store. Depending on the version of the GlassFish, the trusted store is different. The open source version of GlassFish (including the Sun supported Glass Enterprise Server distribution) uses the Java Key Store format. It stores the server's private key and certificates in the `<domain-dir>/config/keystore.jks` file, while the trusted store is `<domain-dir>/config/cacerts.jks`. However, the Enterprise Profile of the GlassFish Server uses the **Network Security Service (NSS)** based key stores and trust store, which are stored at `<domain-dir>/config/key3.db` and `<domain-dir>/config/certs8.db` respectively. The Java Key Store files can be managed using the Java SE's `keytool` utility, while the NSS files are managed using the `certutil` tool.

JDBC realm

With JDBC realm, user credentials can be stored in a relational database table. GlassFish can retrieve user credentials from the realm, and authenticate the user based on the database information and the enabled realm option in the configuration file.

LDAP realm

LDAP is a protocol that allows information about organizations, individuals, and other resources to be organized in a hierarchy. This hierarchical structure allows information to be rapidly retrievable. This read-optimization feature makes LDAP server an ideal authentication realm candidate for large organizations. GlassFish is shipped with an `LDAPRealm` implementation that allows us to configure a realm, based on most LDAP server implementations, such as Sun Java System Directory, Microsoft Active Directory, OpenLDAP, and OpenDS (`http://opends.org`).

Solaris realm

With Solaris realm, the GlassFish Server can be configured to use the Solaris Operating System's user ID and password credentials for authentication. This realm is supported only if GlassFish Server is running on Solaris, version 9 or above (including Open Solaris).

Configuring authentication realms

In this section, we describe how to configure additional authentication realms supported in GlassFish. As the Solaris realm is very easy to configure, and not very commonly used, here, we will focus on configuring the JDBC and LDAP realms.

Configuring a JDBC realm

The JDBC realm uses a JDBC resource to connect to the database that contains the user credentials. Also, the JDBC realm expects the database to have one table that provides the user information, and another for the group information. For example, the following SQL statements can be used to create these tables in the MySQL database.

```
CREATE TABLE  users (
  userid varchar(10) NOT NULL,
  password varchar(40) DEFAULT NULL,
  PRIMARY KEY (userid)
);

CREATE TABLE  groups (
  groupid varchar(20) NOT NULL,
  userid varchar(10) DEFAULT NULL,
  PRIMARY KEY (groupid),
  KEY FK_USERID (userid),
  CONSTRAINT FK_USERID FOREIGN KEY (userid) REFERENCES
  users (userid)
);
```

Once we have created the tables using the above SQL script, the next step is to populate the users and group tables with some data. For security reasons, the JDBC realm does not allow the password to be saved in clear text. Fortunately, most databases have functions that can do string encryption; we can use these utilities to populate the tables. For example, the following statements create two users with the same password `password`, and assign them to two different groups:

```
insert into users (userid, password) values
    ('tom', MD5('password')), ('jerry', MD5('password'));
insert into groups(userid, groupid) values
    ('tom', 'user'), ('jerry', 'manager');
```

Now we can use the Admin Console to create a JDBC realm with the following steps:

1. Log on to the Admin Console.

2. Create a JDBC connection pool and JDBC resource for the database where the user credentials are stored.

3. Navigate to the **Realms** node. Click **New** in the content panel.

4. In the **Class Name** field, select **com.sun.enterprise.security.auth.realm.jdbc. JDBCRealm**.

5. Fill out the form as shown in the following screenshot to create the JDBC realm.

Name: *	MyJDBCRealm
Class Name:	⦿ com.sun.enterprise.security.auth.realm.jdbc.JDBCRealm ▾
	○
	Class name for the realm you want to create

Properties specific to this Class

JAAS context: *	jdbcRealm
JNDI: *	jdbc/Authentication
User Table: *	users
User Name Column: *	userid
Password Column: *	password
Group Table: *	groups
Group Name Column: *	groupid
Assign Group:	
Database User:	
Database Password:	
Digest Algorithm:	MD5
Encoding:	
Charset:	

Note that in this form, once we specify the class name to be JDBCRealm, the **JAAS context** value is automatically set to jdbcRealm. Also, the **Digest Algorithm** is actually a required field. In our example, since the password was encrypted using MD5 algorithm, we need to specify MD5 as the digest algorithm. There are also several optional parameters in this form. For example, the **Assign Group** field can be used to assign all the authenticated users to a specified group. Also, the **Database User** and **Database Password** fields JDBC Realm's connection pool without specifying the authentication credentials as the connection pool definition time. By leaving this information out, other application components will not be able to attempt to query the authentication tables using the connection pool.

Configuring an LDAP realm

The LDAP realm shipped with GlassFish Server can be used with LDAP compliant directory implementations. In this section, let's use the following directory structure as an example and demonstrate how to configure the LDAP realm.

```
dn: dc=programming-stuff,dc=com
objectClass: domain
objectClass: top
dc: programming-stuff

dn: ou=ServiceAccounts,dc=programming-stuff,dc=com
objectClass: organizationalUnit
objectClass: top
ou: ServiceAccounts

dn: cn=JNDIUser,ou=ServiceAccounts,dc=programming-stuff,dc=com
objectClass: person
objectClass: inetOrgPerson
objectClass: organizationalPerson
objectClass: top
givenName: JNDI
uid: JNDIUser
cn: JNDIUser
sn: User

dn: ou=People,dc=programming-stuff,dc=com
objectClass: organizationalunit
objectClass: top
ou: People

dn: uid=tuser1,ou=People,dc=programming-stuff,dc=com
objectClass: person
objectClass: inetOrgPerson
objectClass: organizationalPerson
objectClass: top
givenName: Test
uid: tuser1
cn: tuser1
sn: User1

dn: cn=Architecture,dc=programming-stuff,dc=com
objectClass: groupOfUniqueNames
objectClass: top
cn: Architecture
uniqueMember: uid=tuser1,ou=People,dc=programming-stuff,dc=com
```

This directory defines a top-level domain component, a people container organizational unit that contains all the user accounts, and a group container that specifies the members of the group. Also, this directory structure contains a service account.

> The **LDAP Data Interchange Format** (**LDIF**) file of the sample directory structure is provided in Chapter 7's example bundle, and you can load the LDIF file into a directory server to test the LDAP realm. For an easy-to-use, yet very feature rich LDAP product, you can try the open source OpenDS project, located at `http://opends.org`.

Now we can use the Admin Console to create an LDAP realm with the following steps:

1. Log on to the Admin Console.
2. Navigate to the **Realms** node. Click **New** in the content panel.
3. In the **Class Name** field, select **com.sun.enterprise.security.auth.realm.ldap. LDAPRealm**.
4. Fill out the form as shown in the following screenshot to create the LDAP realm.

Note that in this form, once we specify the class name to be **LDAPRealm**, the JAAS context value is automatically set to **ldapRealm**. The standard properties of the LDAP realm include the following:

- **Directory**: The LDAP URL identifying the directory server
- **Base DN**: The base distinguished name of the user repository
- **Assign Group**: This can be used to assign all the authenticated users to a group

Additional properties include the following:

- `Search-bind-dn` and `search-bind-password`: The credentials of the account with which the LDAP search and other operations are executed.
- `Search-filter`: The search filter used to find the user. The default value is `uid=%s`, meaning the user search will compare the `uid` attribute of a user node with the supplied value.
- `Group-search-filter`: The search filter used to find the group membership for the user. The default value is `uniqueMember=%d`.

Configuring authentication methods for applications

Depending on the type of the application, we use different mechanisms to associate a realm with the application. For example, for web application, the `<realm-name>` element in the `web.xml` deployment descript specifies which realm should be used to authenticate the user.

Besides configuring realms, another factor of authentication is the authentication mechanism. This is particularly important for web applications, which can use one of the following authentication methods supported in GlassFish:

- **BASIC**: Uses the browser's built-in login dialog box to collect user credentials, and transmits the credentials using HTTP headers.
- **FORM**: The application provides its own custom login and error pages.
- **CLIENT-CERT**: The server authenticates the client using a public key certificate. The communication protocol is HTTPS (HTTP over SSL). User-credentialed encryption is SSL.

The authentication method is defined in the `<auth-method>` element of the `web.xml` deployment descriptor.

Using Programmatic login

GlassFish implements an additional security feature, Programmatic login. Programmatic login allows an application to invoke a login method in the application implementation, and the implementation of the login method can use any customized authentication logic. During the invocation of this login method, the GlassFish Server's security infrastructure is not involved. However, a successful login through this method call will result in a `SecurityContext` established for the client as if the client had authenticated using the standard authentication mechanism. Programmatic login is useful when the application has very special authentication requirements that cannot be satisfied by the built-in authentication mechanisms in GlassFish. Programmatic login is supported for servlet, EJB, standalone, or application clients.

Implementing Programmatic login is beyond the scope of this book. For more information, you can refer to the GlassFish Developers Guide.

When we use programmatic login, the `ProgrammaticLoginPermission` permission is required to invoke the programmatic login mechanism for an application, if the security manager is enabled. To grant the required permission to the application, add the following to the `<domain-dir>/config/server.policy` file:

```
grant codeBase "file:<jar-file-path>" {
  permission    com.sun.appserv.security.ProgrammaticLoginPermission
  "login";
};
```

In this case, the `<jar-file-path>` is the path to the application's JAR file, and the `com.sun.appserv.security.ProgrammaticLogin` class enables a user to perform login programmatically.

Each GlassFish Server domain has its own global Java SE policy file, located in `<domain-dir>/config`. The file is named `server.policy`. GlassFish follows the requirements of the Java EE specification, including the presence of the security manager (the Java component that enforces the policy) and a limited permission set for Java EE application code.

Single sign-on

The GlassFish Server supports a limited single sign-on feature. Enabled by default for virtual servers, the single sign-on feature of the GlassFish Server allows multiple web applications deployed to the same virtual server to share the user authentication state. With single sign-on enabled, users who log in to one web application become implicitly logged in to other web applications on the same virtual server that require the same authentication information. Otherwise, users would have to log in separately to each web application whose protected resources they tried to access.

Single sign-on operates according to the following rules:

- Single sign-on applies to web applications configured for the same realm and virtual server. The realm is defined by the realm-name element in the web.xml file. As long as users access only unprotected resources in any of the web applications on a virtual server, they are not challenged to authenticate themselves.

- As soon as a user accesses a protected resource in any web application associated with a virtual server, the user is required to authenticate using the login method defined for the web application currently being accessed.

- After authentication, the roles associated with this user are used for access control decisions across all associated web applications, without challenging the user to authenticate each application individually.

- When the user logs out of one web application, the user's sessions in all web applications are invalidated. Any subsequent attempt to access a protected resource in any application requires the user to authenticate again.

The single sign-on feature utilizes HTTP cookies to transmit a token that associates each request with the saved user identity, so it can only be used in client environments that support cookies. To configure single sign-on, set the following properties in the virtual-server element of the domain.xml file:

- sso-enabled: If false, single sign-on is disabled for this virtual server, and users must authenticate separately to every application on the virtual server. The default is false.

- sso-max-inactive-seconds: Specifies the time after which a user's single sign-on record becomes eligible for purging if no client activity is received. As single sign-on applies across several applications on the same virtual server, access to any of the applications keeps the single sign-on record active. The default value is five minutes (300 seconds). Higher values provide longer single sign-on persistence for the users at the expense of more memory usage on the server.

- sso-reap-interval-seconds: Specifies the interval between purges of expired single sign-on records. The default value is 60.

Here is an example configuration with all default values:

```
<virtual-server id="server" ... >
  ...
  <property name="sso-enabled" value="true"/>
  <property name="sso-max-inactive-seconds" value="300"/>
  <property name="sso-reap-interval-seconds" value="60"/>
</virtual-server>
```

Now that we have seen how to configure user authentication, let's examine how user authorization can be configured in applications and on the GlassFish Server.

Configuring authorization for GlassFish

As we have mentioned, Java EE application authorization is based on roles. Whether an authenticated user can access a resource or not depends on where the user's security principal or group membership can be mapped to an authorized role.

GlassFish uses server-specific deployment descriptors to manage the mapping between users/groups in a realm and roles in an application, and the authorization is based on application roles. The following example shows a `security-role-mapping` element in the `sun-web.xml` deployment descriptor for a web application.

```
<sun-web-app>
  <security-role-mapping>
    <role-name>User</role-name>
    <principal-name>tom</principal-name>
    <principal-name>jerry</principal-name>
    <group-name>MouseAndCat</group-name>
  </security-role-mapping>
  <security-role-mapping>
    <role-name>Admin</role-name>
    <principal-name>adminuser</principal-name>
  </security-role-mapping>
</sun-web-app>
```

Using default principals and role mappings

In practice, it is quite common for many organizations and developers to think about role-based access control as group-based. For example, when we build a Java EE web application, we may want to build the access control based on LDAP or AD groups to which an employee belongs. Effectively, each group should be mapped to a role with the same name. While we can add this type of "identity mapping" to the deployment descriptor, it can be extremely tedious.

To address this issue, GlassFish server provides a default principal to role mapping mechanism. The default mapping indeed maps groups to roles of the same name. Furthermore, we can also provide a customized class to modify the mapping.

We can set the default principal to role mapping as follows.

```
# cd $AS_INSTALL/bin

# ./asadmin set server.security-service.activate-default-principal-to-
role-mapping=true

# ./asadmin set server.security-service.mapped-principal-class=CustomPrin
cipalImplClass
```

Configuring certificates and secure communication protocols

Digital certificates enable secure and confidential communication between two entities. There are different kinds of certificates. Personal certificates are used by individuals. Server certificates are used to establish secure sessions between the server and clients through secure sockets layer (SSL) technology.

Digital certificates are typically issued by a trusted third party called a **Certification Authority (CA)**, such as VeriSign. Once a CA has issued a certificate, the holder can present it as proof of identity and to establish encrypted, confidential communications. In addition to the public key, a certificate typically includes information such as the following:

- The name of the holder and other identification, such as the URL of the web server using the certificate, or an individual's e-mail address
- The name of the CA that issued the certificate
- An expiration date

Most common server products and client applications are typically configured to accept certificates issued by well known CAs. However, there is a cost associated with these certificates. Due to this, many companies adopt different tools and use them as internal CAs, and they use these internal CAs to issue certificates. As long as the communication parties agree to trust these internal CAs, the communication can be equally secure and effective.

GlassFish is preconfigured with a keystore and trust store. As we have seen before, depending on the distribution of GlassFish, the keystore and trust stores are different; while most distributions use the Java key store, the enterprise distribution uses NSS. In this chapter, we focus on the utility for managing the Java based key stores — the `keytool` utility. For detailed discussion on NSS key stores, you can refer to the GlassFish Server Developer Guide.

Working with the keytool utility

In this section, we discuss how we can use the `keytool` utility to generate keys and create certificates. Refer to the Java SE security documentation for more information: `http://java.sun.com/javase/6/docs/technotes/guides/security/index.html`.

First, we can use the the following command to generate a new certificate in the `keystore` file, `keystore.jks`:

```
# cd $AS_INSTALL/domains/domain1/config
# keytool -genkey -alias keyAlias -keyalg RSA -keypass changeit -
storepass changeit -keystore keystore.jks
```

The `-genKey` command uses any unique name as your `keyAlias`. A prompt appears that asks for your name, organization, and other information. Once we answer all the questions, the `keytool` utility generates a key pair, and creates a server certificate using the generated public key, and user provided information.

Now, export the generated certificate to a `server.cer` file:

```
# cd $AS_INSTALL/domains/domain1/config
# keytool -export -alias keyAlias -storepass changeit -file  server.cer
-keystore keystore.jks
```

Next, import the certificate into the local key store and, if necessary, the local trust store using the following command format:

```
# cd $AS_INSTALL/domains/domain1/config
# keytool -import -v -trustcacerts -alias keyAlias -file server.cer -
keystore cacerts.jks -keypass changeit -storepass changeit
```

Now, we have created a new pair of keys and we got a self-signed certificate created using the generated public key, and we loaded the keys and certificates into the GlassFish Server key store and trust store. In the next section, we present how to use the new certificate to configure SSL and TLS support.

SSL and TLS support

The GlassFish Server supports the SSL 3.0 and the TLS 1.0 encryption protocols. To use SSL, GlassFish Server must have a certificate for each external interface or IP address that accepts secure connections.

A cipher is a cryptographic algorithm used for encryption or decryption. SSL and TLS protocols support a variety of ciphers used to authenticate the server and client to each other, transmit certificates, and establish session keys.

Some ciphers are stronger and more secure than others. Clients and servers can support different cipher suites. During a secure connection, the client and the server agree to use the strongest cipher that they both have enabled for communication, so it is usually sufficient to enable all ciphers.

Configuring SSL and TLS

By default, HTTPS is enabled on port 8181 for web traffic, and SSL is enabled on ports 3820 and 3902 for IIOP traffic. The server certificate used to enable these protocols has an alias slas, and it was created and used to populate the key store and trust store. In the previous section, we created a new certificate; let's see how we can configure HTTPS and SSL using the newly created certificate. We will use HTTP listener as an example to demonstrate how to do this. Configuring SSL for IIOP using the new certificate follows almost the same process.

The following steps summarize the action:

1. Log on to the Admin Console.
2. Expand the **Configuration** node, and then expand the **HTTP Service** and **HTTP Listeners** nodes.
3. Click **http-listener-2**, and click the **SSL** tab in the main content panel, as shown in the following screenshot.
4. Change the **Certificate NickName** field value to the key alias name **slas**.
5. Make necessary changes to the cipher suites supported for the **HTTP Listener**.
6. Click **Save**, and restart GlassFish.

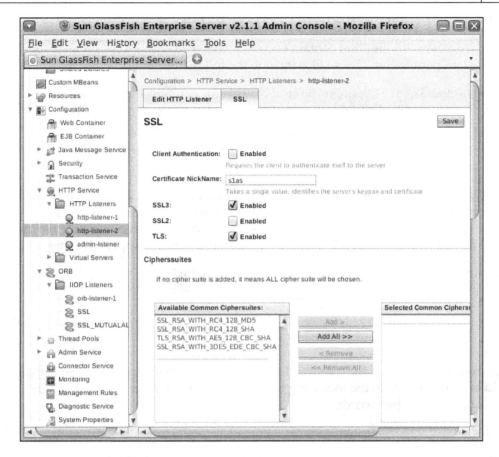

Additional security concerns in GlassFish

In this section, we discuss several additional security features implemented in GlassFish, and some common practices we take to make GlassFish more secure.

First, let's consider the management of passwords in GlassFish.

Administering passwords

GlassFish uses two categories of passwords—those necessary for running the administration and configuration tasks, and those necessary for configuring the resources. Examples of administration related passwords include the GlassFish master password, and the administrator's password. Examples of application resource related passwords include the passwords for a data source.

Working with administration related passwords

Encoded password files that contain encoded passwords need to be protected using file system permissions. These files include the following:

- `<domain-dir>/master-password`: This file contains the encoded master password and should be protected with filesystem permissions 600.

- Any password file created to pass as an argument by using the `--passwordfile` argument to the `asadmin` utility should be protected with filesystem permissions 600.

Instead of typing the password at the command line, you can access the password for a command from a file. The `--passwordfile` option of the `asadmin` utility takes the name of the file that contains the passwords. The entry for a password in the file must have the `AS_ADMIN_` prefix followed by the password name in uppercase letters.

The following other types of passwords can be specified:

- `AS_ADMIN_MASTERPASSWORD`
- `AS_ADMIN_USERPASSWORD`
- `AS_ADMIN_ALIASPASSWORD`

For example, to specify the password for the domain administration server (DAS), add an entry similar to the following to the password file, where `adminadmin` is the administrator password:

```
AS_ADMIN_PASSWORD=adminadmin
```

If `AS_ADMIN_PASSWORD` has been exported to the global environment, specifying the `--passwordfile` option will produce a warning about using the `--passwordfile` option.

Encrypting application resources related passwords

By default, when we configure a resource, such as a JDBC connection pool, its configuration, including the password, is saved in the `domain.xml` file in clear text. For example:

```
<jdbc-connection-pool ...>
  <property name="user" value="user"/>
  <property name="password" value="mypassword"/>
  <property name="portNumber" value="3306"/>
  <property name="databaseName" value="glassfish"/>
  <property name="serverName" value="localhost"/>
</jdbc-connection-pool>
```

Even though we can protect the `domain.xml` file at the operating system level by removing read access from most developers, this may not be compliant with an organization's security policy, such as "No password should be saved in clear text".

GlassFish provides a very straightforward solution to this problem. We can use the `asadmin` CLI's `create-password-alias` command to produce a password alias. For example, for the password value we just saw, we can create a password alias as follows:

```
# cd $AS_INSTALL/bin
# ./asadmin create-password-alias myalias
```

When the command prompts for the password value, we need to enter the clear text value twice.

The `create-password-alias` command uses the master password to encrypt the clear text password value, and saves the encrypted passwords in `domain-passwords` file under the GlassFish Server configuration directory. Each encrypted password is keyed by the password alias, and whenever the configuration file references the password alias, GlassFish decrypts the password on the fly.

Due to this, we can change the previous connection pool definition as follows:

```xml
<jdbc-connection-pool ...>
  <property name="user" value="user"/>
  <property name="password" value="${ALIAS=myalias}"/>
  <property name="portNumber" value="3306"/>
  <property name="databaseName" value="glassfish"/>
  <property name="serverName" value="localhost"/>
</jdbc-connection-pool>
```

Java ACC support

Java Authorization Contract for Containers (JACC) is the part of the Java EE specification that defines an interface for pluggable authorization providers. JACC providers use the **Java Authentication and Authorization Service (JAAS)** APIs, which enables the services to authenticate and enforce access controls upon users. JAAS implements a Java technology version of the standard **Pluggable Authentication Module (PAM)** framework.

The GlassFish Server provides a simple file-based JACC-compliant authorization engine as a default JACC provider, named `default`. An alternate provider named `simple` is also provided. To configure an alternate provider using the Administration Console, open the **Security** component under the relevant configuration, and select the **JACC Providers** component.

Auditing

GlassFish Server uses audit modules to capture audit trails of all authentication and authorization decisions. GlassFish Server provides a default audit module, as well as the ability to customize the audit modules.

The following commands of the `asadmin` CLI utility allow us to manage audit modules for the add-on component that implements the audit capabilities.

- `create-audit-module`
- `list-audit-modules`
- `delete-audit-module`

Audit modules collect and store information on incoming requests (servlets, EJB components) and outgoing responses. You can create a custom audit module.

To specify an audit module using the Administration Console, open the **Security** component under the relevant configuration, and select the **Audit Modules** component. For details, click the **Help** button in the Administration Console.

Summary

This chapter provided an introduction to the GlassFish Server's security features. It also described how you can secure the Glass Server environment, and the applications deployed to it. At this point, you should be comfortable with the big picture of GlassFish Server's security model, and you should also be able to configure GlassFish to address common security concerns.

Security is always an ever-changing field. Currently, with more and more efforts being put in integrating many heterogeneous systems together, many new technology, standards and products have emerged to address the security issues in these scenarios. For example, the OpenSSO project (`http://opensso.org`) implements an extensible identity and access management service that supports many advanced features such as pluggable web service security, cross domain single sign-on. OpenSSO can be easily integrated with the GlassFish Server to enhance the security capability. We strongly encourage you to spend time and efforts in getting familiar with these types of solutions and products.

This chapter concluded the coverage of the essential services and capabilities of the GlassFish Server. The rest of this book focuses on configuring and managing the GlassFish Server for large-scale deployment. In the next chapter, we will discuss how multiple GlassFish Server instances can be clustered to improve its throughput and availability.

8
Monitoring GlassFish

In this chapter, we discuss the monitoring features implemented in GlassFish, and introduce several very useful utilities that we can use to further improve our ability to monitor GlassFish. The goal of this chapter is to help you get familiar with these features and tools so that you can monitor, and ultimately maintain the GlassFish Server runtime.

Monitoring features of GlassFish

GlassFish provides extensive capabilities for monitoring its runtime environment. The monitoring service of GlassFish can be used to gather detailed statistics of the underlying JVM and application components deployed to GlassFish. The information gathered through monitoring is critical for discovering potential issues, troubleshooting, and performance tuning.

In this section, we first describe the GlassFish monitoring service, and then show you how to start monitoring GlassFish.

Understanding the GlassFish monitoring service

The GlassFish monitoring service monitors most of the main components and services of the server environment. The following list describes their main monitorable properties:

- **JVM Software**: The uptime, JVM memory and garbage collection system, and class loading sub system.
- **HTTP Service**: The total connections, keep alive connections, file cache status, and the HTTP listener status.

- **JMS Connector Services**: The JMS connection factory's statistics on connections created, available connections, and so on.

- **The system ORB**: The number of IIOP connections to the GlassFish **Object Request Broker (ORB)**.

- **Web Container**: The HTTP listeners' request processing statistics, sessions created, JSP page translation, and so on.

- **EJB Container**: The number of EJB instances created and destroyed; EJB method invocation statistics, and so on.

- **JDBC Connection Pool**: The number of connections created and destroyed; connection wait time, and so on.

- **Thread Pool**: The total thread count, live threads, and individual thread status.

- **Transaction Service**: The number of committed and rolled-back transactions and the transaction service status.

Each subsystem has a different list of statistics that can be obtained. By default, the monitoring service on all these subsystems is turned off. We need to enable monitoring in order to gather necessary statistics. In GlassFish, the monitoring capability for each subsystem can be enabled or disabled independent of other subsystems using the `asadmin` CLI utility or the Admin Console.

The following three monitoring levels are supported by GlassFish: OFF, LOW, and HIGH. Monitoring can be disabled by changing the level to OFF. When the component's monitoring level is LOW or HIGH, the component and its subtypes become monitorable and it is up to the component to make the distinction with regard to the interpretation of the levels. For example, an EJB method is only monitorable when the monitoring level of the EJB container is HIGH, whereas the transaction service cannot make any distinction between HIGH and LOW. Monitoring levels can be dynamically changed at runtime. The level changes are recorded in the `domain.xml` file and remain active until they are changed at a later time.

 Monitoring is instantiated on first usage. After the resource or connection pool is used, the statistics show up. For example, if we use the JDBC API resource and get a result set, the monitoring values are only shown after a resource or pool has been accessed at least once.

Configuring monitoring

When GlassFish is first installed, the monitoring level for all the subsystems is set to OFF, and none of the monitoring statistics are collected. To enable the monitoring on the subsystems, we can use the Admin Console. The following steps can be used to enable monitoring:

1. Log on to the Admin Console.
2. Expand the **Configuration** node in the navigation panel.
3. Click **Monitoring**.

The Admin Console displays the current monitoring service settings, as shown in the following screenshot.

4. In the main panel, set the monitoring levels for all subsystems to **HIGH**, and click **Save**.

 In this chapter, we set all the monitoring levels to **HIGH** for demonstration purposes, because this monitoring level is guaranteed to collect most of the statistics. In practice, you should set the level more appropriately to reduce the performance overhead. For a detailed description of each monitor-able subsystem and the statistics collected, please refer to the *GlassFish Server Administration Guide*.

We can also set the monitoring level using the `set` command of the `asadmin` CLI. For example, if we wanted to set the monitoring level for the JVM to **HIGH**, we would enter the following command:

```
# cd $AS_INSTALL/bin
# ./asadmin set server.monitoring-service.module-monitoring-levels.
jvm=HIGH
```

Now that we have enabled monitoring, let's look at how to view the monitoring data. In order to access the monitoring data, we can use several tools. Some of the tools are built into the GlassFish Server, and several additional tools are also available. In the next section, let's examine the tools available within GlassFish.

Using built-in monitoring tools

In this section, we discuss the monitoring tools built into GlassFish. First, let's understand how to view the monitoring data in GlassFish.

Viewing monitoring data

Once the monitoring service is enabled, we can view the monitoring data for the monitorable subsystem using Admin Console or the `asadmin` CLI utility. The following steps show how to use the Admin Console to view the monitoring data:

1. Log on to the Admin Console.
2. Click **Application Server** in the navigation pane.

3. Click the **Monitor** tab in the main content pane, as shown in the following screenshot.

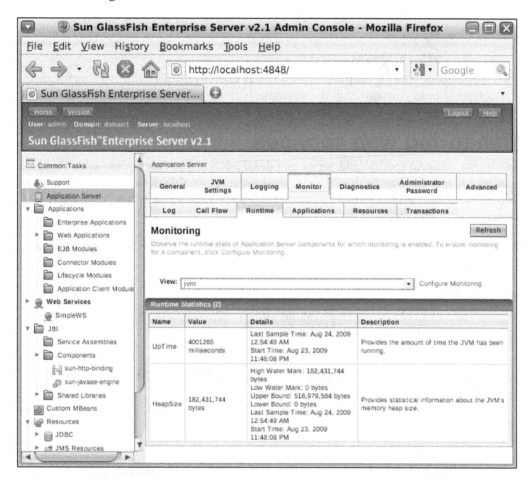

The screenshot shows the monitoring data for the JVM, such as the uptime and the object heap size. This user interface allows you to easily view other monitoring data. For example, if you want to view the monitoring data for a particular JDBC connection pool, simply click the **Resources** tab, and then select the target connection pool from the **View** drop-down menu.

The `get` command of the `asadmin` CLI allows us to view the monitoring data. This feature can be useful if you need to build your own monitoring and alert scripts. In the following example, we retrieve the monitoring statistics for the JVM:

```
# cd $AS_INSTALL/bin
# ./asadmin get -m server.jvm.*
```

The `-m` option, or its long format, `--monitor` is used to retrieve the monitoring data. The output should contain similar information as we see in the Admin Console.

Monitoring web services

Besides the general monitoring services, GlassFish also provides some additional features for monitoring deployed web services. If we enable detailed monitoring for web services, we can track operational statistics for web services, and can display messages sent and received by web services.

To enable detailed monitoring on web services, configure the web service with the following steps:

1. Log on to the Admin Console.

2. Expand the **Web Services** node in the navigation pane, and click the web service you want to enable monitoring.

3. Click the **Monitor** tab in the main content pane.

4. Click the **Configuration** tab, set the **Monitoring** level to **HIGH**, as shown in the following screenshot.

5. Click **Save**.

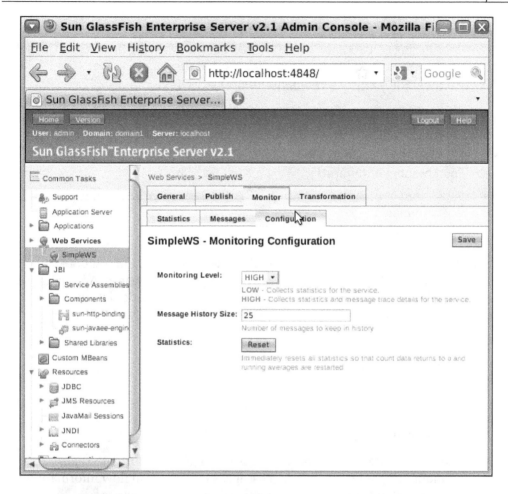

The **Monitoring Levels** for web services monitoring are defined as follows:

- **LOW**: Monitors response time, throughput, total number of requests, faults, and monitoring of number of requests per second, average response time, and throughput attributes for the web service.

- **HIGH**: In addition to the metrics monitored at **LOW** level, this also monitors SOAP request and response messages.

- **OFF**: Disables monitoring.

 We can also configure web service monitoring with the `configure-webservice-management` command of the `asadmin` CLI.

Viewing web service statistics

To view monitoring statistics for a web service, simply log on to the Admin Console, navigate to the target **Web Service**, and click the **Monitor** tab. The **Statistics** tab in the content pane shows the following information:

- Response time in milliseconds on any successful or unsuccessful operation (maximum, minimum, and average)
- Throughput
- Total number of requests
- Total number of faults, including URI of the endpoint where the fault originated
- Viewing web service messages

We can also click the **Messages** tab to view the detailed request and response messages. By default, the Admin Console retains the last 25 messages. Admin Console displays details of SOAP requests and responses, and HTTP header information. In addition, the following information is displayed for a web service request:

- Remote username
- Client host information
- Timestamp
- Response information (success or failure)
- Size of the request

We can also select a filter to view only success messages or failure messages. If call flow monitoring is enabled, each message is linked to call flow information that enables you to look at the call stack information for each message.

Using the Call Flow analysis

The Call Flow service allows us to monitor method calls as they flow through various containers in the Application Server and application code. This is useful to both the application developer and the server administrator. This information can be extremely useful for troubleshooting and performance tuning, as it visualizes the method call stack.

Call Flow has intimate knowledge of the container and the performance impact is very low. It collects runtime information about an application, such as the user principal, transaction ID, application name, method name, exceptions, and the time spent in various containers. A call is monitored as it flows through various containers in GlassFish and through the user application code.

By default, the Call Flow service is turned off. It can be turned on using Admin Console or the `asadmin` utility. To do this, complete the following steps:

1. Log on to the Admin Console.
2. Click **Application Server** in the navigation panel, and then click the **Monitor** tab.
3. Click the **Call Flow** tab.
4. Check the **Call Flow Monitoring** box to enable call flow.

    The Call Flow form also allows us to further customize the call flow service. For example, we can specify which user's request calls are monitored, and we can also limit the source IP address from which a user's request processing call flows are stored.
5. Click **Save**.

Once GlassFish has been set up with Call Flow service, we can view the Call flow data collected. To do this, repeat the previous steps until we see the Call Flow tab. Now we are able to see a list of request-initiated call flow data.

If we click on any one of them, the Call Flow Details page appears, as shown in the following screenshot. As we can see, the Call Flow details include an illustration of the call stack, and the percentage of the time that the request processing spent within each application layer.

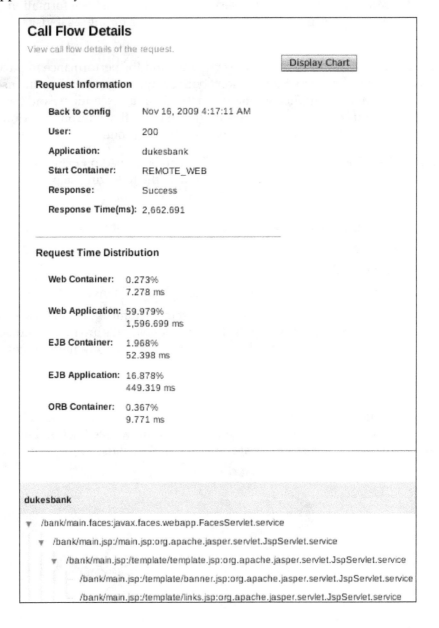

Using self management rules

Application Server administrators can use the management rules feature to set policies that self-configure and self-tune the connection pool or ORB thread pool, detect thread or server hangs, manage memory leaks and out of memory errors, and manage disk usage. This feature allows Application Server to do the following:

- Manage complexity through self-configuration
- Improve ease-of-use by automating mundane management tasks
- Improve performance by self-tuning in unpredictable runtime conditions
- Improve availability by preventing and recovering from failures
- Improve security by taking self-protective actions when security threats are detected

Self management rules

Self management in GlassFish is built on a simple concept of management rules. A management rule is built using the standard JMX infrastructure. The rule has two parts: an event to be detected, and an optional action to be performed upon detecting the event. The configuration is a set of rules specified by the user. The information is populated in the GlassFish configuration file, domain.xml.

The events that are to be detected and their corresponding actions are included in the management configuration set.

The event model is based on the JMX notification mechanism. All events are subclasses of JMX notification. Events are classified into three types: predefined events, monitor events, and notification events. The Application Server provides a set of predefined events, which can trigger a rule to be executed. The predefined event types are described in the next section.

There are six predefined event types for self management rules. They are as follows:

- **Monitor events**: Provide the capability to monitor an attribute of an MBean.
- **Notification events**: A generic event notification mechanism. Any custom MBean that can emit a notification can be a notification event.
- **Lifecycle events**: Provide the capability to configure a management rule based on the Application Server's lifecycle state (ready, shutdown, termination).
- **Log events**: Provide log records and other relevant logging data to the action as userData of the notification.

- **Trace events**: Provide request ID, component name, and other useful tracing data to the action as userData of the notification.

- **Timer events**: Provide useful timer data to the action as userData of the notification.

Configuring management rules

The management rules node in the Admin Console displays the list of existing rules in a tree view. When a rule node is clicked, the main content panel shows the details related to that rule.

Management Rules can be also be created using the Admin Console. To do this, click the **Management Node** in the navigation panel, and then click **New** in the content panel. The following screenshot shows the first step of the management rule creation process in the Admin Console. The second step varies depending on the **Event Type** selected here.

To configure management rules from the command line, use the create-management-rule command. The command syntax is as follows:

```
# cd #AS_INSTALL/bin

# ./asadmin create-management-rule --ruleenabled=true --action action-
mbean-name -eventtype <event-type> rule-name
```

Management rules are very useful. For example, we can use management rules to define alerts on resource conditions, such as when the server memory usage is exceeding a predefined percentage. In fact, for Sun customers with commercial support, Sun provides a performance advisor tool for performance tuning and system resource usage alerts. The alert mechanism of the performance advisor is actually based on management rules discussed in this section. We will discuss the performance advisor tool in detail in Chapter 10, *Troubleshooting and Tuning GlassFish*.

Monitoring GlassFish with other utilities

As the monitoring service's capabilities are built based on JMX and J2EE management standards, many tools, both open source and proprietary, can be used to further monitor GlassFish. In this section, we first introduce the JConsole utility bundled with the JDK software since version 5.0, and show you how JConsole can be used to monitor GlassFish. We then discuss the monitoring and management tool suits (called the GlassFish Enterprise Manager) provided by Sun to customers who purchased the commercial support for GlassFish. Finally, we briefly discuss how to use other tools to monitor GlassFish.

Monitoring GlassFish using JConsole

The Java Monitoring and Management Console (JConsole) is a utility bundled with the JDK software since version 5.0. It provides a GUI-based client that is capable of monitoring and managing JMX-based remote systems, such as GlassFish. Some of the monitoring capabilities it provides are as follows:

- Low memory detection
- Garbage collection enablement and disablement
- Class loader traces
- Deadlock detection
- Control of log levels
- Access to operating system resources
- Management of an application's MBeans

To use the JConsole utility, follow the given steps:

1. Start it by running `$JDK_HOME/bin/jconsole`.

2. In the **New Connection** dialog, select **Remote Process**, enter the information as shown in the following screenshot, and click **Connect**.

 When you enter the information as shown in the previous screenshot, the remote process refers to the GlassFish Server process running on your server machine. The port 8686 is the default JMX port for GlassFish. The user credential should authenticate a user in the admin group.

The following screenshot contains a detailed view of the monitoring data available through the JConsole.

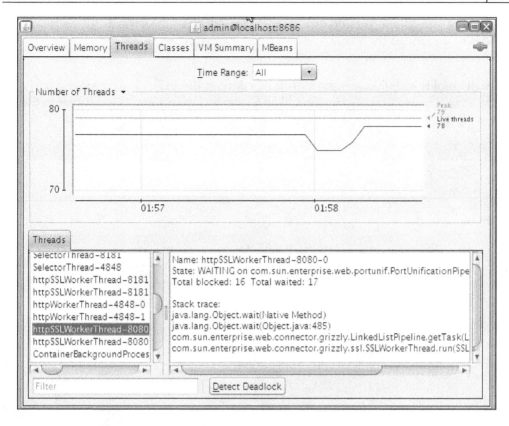

Using the VisualVM tool

Based on the NetBeans platform, VisualVM (`https://visualvm.dev.java.net`) is another JMX-based monitoring tool that can provide a detailed view into the JVM. In this section, we discuss how to install VisualVM, and how to use it.

> In fact, recent releases of the Sun JDK 6 software include VisualVM as a built-in tool. If you do have a recent version of Sun's JDK 6, you can start it by running the `jvisualvm` command in the `bin` directory of the JDK installation. However, we strongly recommend you to download and install the standalone version of the tool, and use it for monitoring Java applications. The reason is that the standalone version is very up-to-date, and you can take advantage of many new features and capability of VisualVM.

Installing a standalone version of VisualVM is very straightforward. All we need to do is to download the VisualVM tool from the project website, and unzip the downloaded file to a working directory.

Once the tool is installed, we can start it by running the `visualvm` command in the `<visualvm_install>/bin` directory. The VisualVM user interface is shown in the following screenshot.

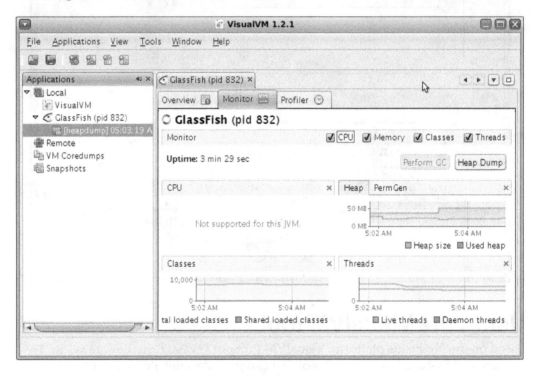

As we can see, once VisualVM is started, it first searches for the locally running JVM processes. For example, if we run the tool on the same server that hosts our running GlassFish Server, it automatically adds the JVM process as a local process. We can also manually add a remote GlassFish instance through a JMX connection. To add a remote GlassFish Server, complete the following steps:

1. Right-click the **Remote** node, select **Add Remote Host**.

2. Enter a remote host name in the dialog, and click **OK**.

3. Right-click the remote host node you just added, and select **Add JMX Connection**.

4. Enter the remote GlassFish Server's JMX connection information, and the administrator credentials. Click **OK**.

If the information for the remote GlassFish Server is correct, the VisualVM utility should be able to connect to the GlassFish, and start monitoring it. Out of the box, the VisualVM tool allows us to view the overall status of the GlassFish Server's JVM process. It also allows us to monitor JVM's CPU usage, running threads, class loading, and so on.

VisualVM also has several plugins that we can use. This plugins can be installed as follows:

1. Select **Plugins** from the **Tools** menu. The **Plugins** dialog should appear, as shown in the following screenshot.

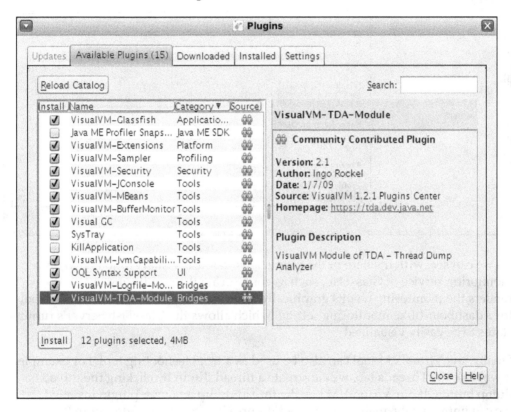

2. In the **Plugins** dialog, select the plugins we want to install and click the **Install** button.

    Notice the Glassfish plugin. The Glassfish plugin makes the monitorable properties accessible to the VisualVM user interface.

3. Accept the license agreement, and wait for the installation process to finish. Restart VisualVM, and the new plugins are ready to use.

After installing the plugins, VisualVM has more capabilities, as shown in the following screenshot.

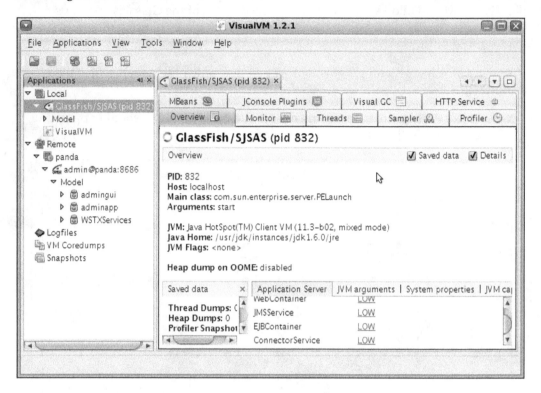

As we can see, with the help of the plugins, we can use VisualVM to manage the monitoring service of GlassFish, such as configuring the monitoring levels. It also renders the monitoring results graphically. This makes VisualVM an excellent tool for a dashboard-like monitoring setting, which allows the GlassFish Server's runtime status to be easily visualized.

Finally, the VirtualVM tool can also be used as a troubleshooting tool. For example, if we click the **Threads** tab, we can create a thread dump by clicking the thread dump button. If our VirtualVM has the thread dump analyzer plugin installed, we can immediately analyze the thread dump. Chapter 10 provides more information on troubleshooting.

Using GlassFish Enterprise Manager for monitoring

The GlassFish Enterprise Manager is a suite of monitoring, managing, and tuning tools provided by Sun to customers who have purchased commercial support for GlassFish. One of the tools included in the Enterprise Manager is the Performance Monitor. The Performance Monitor is built on top of VisualVM, and it provides a precise and focused monitoring tool for GlassFish. In this section, let's see how to use it, and compare it with the open source version of the VisualVM plus the GlassFish plugin.

> The Enterprise Manager also includes two other tools. The performance advisor provides a simple yet effective tool for tuning the GlassFish Server, and we will discuss how to use it in Chapter 10. The SNMP Monitor allows the monitor-able properties of GlassFish to be accessible through the SNMP. Installing and configuring SNMP monitor is quite straightforward, and we won't discuss it in this book. If you are interested, you can refer to the *SNMP Monitor Installation and Quick Start Guide*, located at
> `http://docs.sun.com/app/docs/doc/820-7189`.

Installing the Performance Monitor is straightforward, all we need to do is download the enterprise manager patch ZIP file and extract the included `glassfish-perf-monitor.zip` file. After this, we can start the performance monitor by running the `glassfishpm` command.

The Enterprise Monitor user interface is shown in the following screenshot.

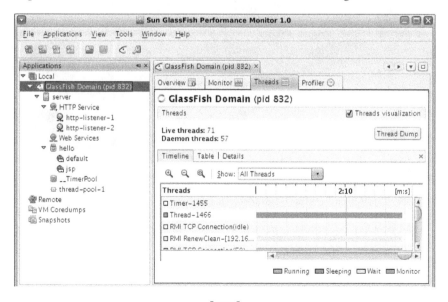

As we can see, the performance monitor organizes the monitorable entities of GlassFish in a tree hierarchy, including the virtual HTTP server with HTTP listeners server configuration. For each entity, the performance monitor collects very detailed monitoring data, and renders the monitoring result graphically. For example, for HTTP listeners, the performance monitor shows all the monitorable properties, includes the number of requests handled, number of concurrent connections, and so on.

Comparing the performance monitor with VisualVM and its open source GlassFish plugin, we think the performance monitor is better suited to monitor GlassFish in a mission-critical environment. We hope the open source GlassFish plugin for VisualVM will continue to improve, and become a viable monitoring tool for all the GlassFish deployment.

Summary

Without these monitoring features and utilities, it is difficult to ensure that GlassFish is working efficiently, or even properly. If you are planning a production deployment of GlassFish, you should definitely consider how you will monitor it, and what tools you will use so that you can discover any potential issues of the environment quickly. This chapter provides you with some essential information that can help you achieve this goal.

9
Configuring Clusters and High Availability

In this chapter, we will discuss how to configure clusters for the GlassFish Server, and use a load balancer to distribute load across the server instances in the cluster. We will also discuss the **High Availability (HA)** options supported by GlassFish, and how to enable HA. The goal of this chapter is to help you gain the knowledge necessary for planning and creating a production-ready GlassFish Server deployment.

Configuring clusters for GlassFish

In order to deliver the required performance, throughput, and reliability, a production environment typically needs to host enterprise applications using multiple running application server instances. In order to easily configure and maintain these server instances, most application server products, including GlassFish, allow these server instances to be grouped into a cluster and administered together. In this section, we first review the core concepts of the GlassFish cluster, and then show you how to configure and manage clusters.

Understanding GlassFish clusters

A GlassFish cluster is a logical entity that groups multiple GlassFish Server instances. The server instances within a cluster can run on different physical machines or on the same machine. The cluster is administered by the **Domain Administration Server (DAS)**. The server instances in a cluster share the same configuration, and they host all applications and resources deployed to the cluster.

The main benefit of a cluster is that it significantly simplifies the administration of server instances. Instead of configuring these server instances and deploying applications to them individually, a cluster provides a one-stop administration facility to enforce the homogeneity of server instances. Besides, a cluster provides very good support for horizontal scalability. For example, if the production environment no longer has sufficient processing power, we can dynamically create a GlassFish Server instance and add it to the existing cluster without extensive reconfiguration. Finally, with the help of a load balancer and appropriate HA configuration, a cluster can be made resilient to server instance issues.

 We will focus on the clustering aspect of GlassFish in this section. Load balancers and HA will be discussed later in this chapter.

The following figure illustrates the main components of a cluster from the administration perspective.

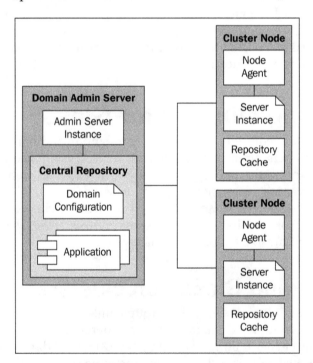

The components illustrated in the figure are described as follows:

- The Domain Administration Server (DAS): DAS is a special server instance responsible for administration of a domain. All administrative operations are routed to DAS. Upon receiving administrative requests, DAS is responsible for sending the request to an individual server instance, or broadcasting it to all the server instances in a cluster. DAS can administer server instances running on remote hosts as well.

- Node agent: A node agent is a light-weight process running on the physical server that hosts GlassFish Server instances. The node agent is responsible for managing the life cycle of these server instances. It can perform the following tasks:

    ° Start, stop, restart, create, and delete server instances

    ° Provide a view of the log files of failed server instance

 If the node agent crashes, it does not affect the server instances and user applications that are currently running. However, a failed node agent can no longer manage and monitor those server instances.

- Server instance: With the exception of DAS, all the other server instances must be created with a reference to a node agent. A server instance can be stand-alone, or it can belong to a cluster. A stand-alone instance maintains and uses its own configuration, while a clustered instance inherits majority of the configuration information from the cluster.

 In our experience, stand-alone server instances are rarely used. Even if you only need one server instance to host applications, we recommend that you define a cluster with only one instance. This approach always allows the server to be potentially scaled out by adding additional server instances to the cluster. The overhead of clustered instance is completely negligible.

- The central repository and repository cache: The central repository is maintained by DAS. The central repository contains the server instance configuration data, and the applications deployed to the GlassFish domain. Each server instance and cluster synchronizes the central repository to its local repository cache. Keep in mind that the repository cache is a subset of the central repository, because the server instance and cluster only synchronize the information pertinent to itself.

> The local repository cache makes it possible to keep stand-alone and clustered server instances running while DAS is shut down. In fact, many organizations indeed shut down DAS in production environment, and they only start up the DAS when there is a new deployment of applications or resources. Without the DAS running, the GlassFish configuration cannot be changed using common administrative tasks.

A node agent is associated with a particular domain when it is created, and it can service only a single domain. If a physical machine hosts server instances that belong to multiple domains, it must run multiple node agents, one for each domain.

DAS only needs the node agent to perform administrative operations on the server instances. The synchronization between DAS and server instances takes place directly through the JMX API remote connector.

The server instance or node agent synchronizes its state with the central repository in the following cases: completely at instance or node agent creation and start-up time, and incrementally as configuration changes are made to the central repository.

Now let's dive into the process of configuring a GlassFish cluster.

Configuring clusters

In this section, we discuss the necessary steps to configure a GlassFish cluster, and along the way we will discuss more features of the GlassFish cluster.

> GlassFish clusters can be created on most operating system and hardware platforms. The noticeable exceptions are Microsoft Windows running the 64-bit JDK software, and Mac OSX.

Obtaining cluster support

The very first thing we need to do in order to configure a cluster is to make sure that the GlassFish Server we are working with has cluster support. Earlier, we introduced the concept of the usage profile of GlassFish. As it turned out, clustering support is available in the cluster and enterprise profiles, and not in the developer profile by default. However, even if we originally installed GlassFish in the developer profile, we can easily upgrade the GlassFish Server to enable clustering support. To do this, complete the following steps:

1. Log on to the GlassFish Admin Console.
2. Click the **Application Server** node in the navigation pane.
3. Click the **General** tab in the main content pane.
4. Click **Add Cluster Support**, as shown in the following screenshot.
5. Click **OK** to confirm the choice.
6. Restart the GlassFish Server.

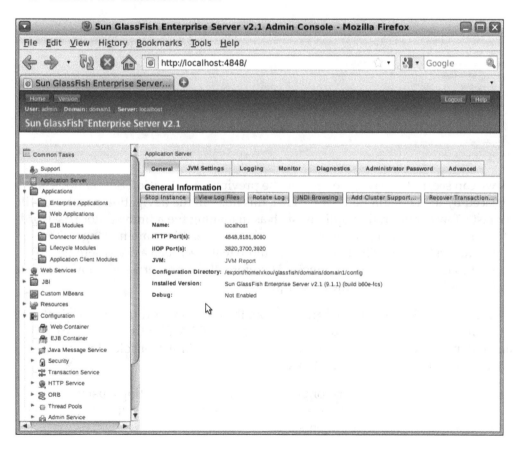

Once GlassFish restarts, we can log on to the Admin Console. We can confirm the cluster support by verifying the new Admin Console, as shown in the following screenshot.

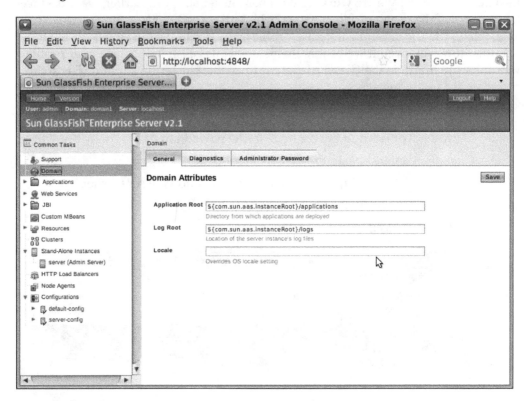

As we can see, in the navigation panel, the previous **Application Server** node is replaced by the **Domain** node. If we click this node in the navigation panel, we will see just a few configuration options, such as managing the administrator password. Most of the other management options, such as JVM settings are no longer there in the Admin Console. The reason is that those features, such as JVM settings are applied to individual server instances. Therefore, these properties are now associated with the server instances in the cluster profile.

For a GlassFish Server that is upgraded from the developer profile, the original server instance now becomes the DAS instance and GlassFish treats the DAS as a stand-alone server instance. When we log on to the Admin Console, this server is listed under the **Stand-Alone Instances** node.

Once we have enabled clusters for GlassFish, we can start creating clusters. As all server instances are managed through node agents, the next step in creating a cluster is to create and start the node agents.

Creating node agents

We can create a node agent in two ways: using the Admin Console, or the
`create-node-agent` command of the `asadmin` CLI. The following screenshot
shows the Admin Console user interface for creating a node agent.

As you can see in the screenshot, to create a node agent using the Admin Console,
simply click **Node Agents** in the navigation panel, enter the name of the node agent
in the content panel, and click **OK**.

The node agent created using the Admin Console is merely a place holder. The
Admin Console shows the status of the newly created node agent as "Waiting
for rendezvous". In other words, at this point the node agent is created from the
administration perspective and we can go on and perform additional configuration,
such as defining server instances for the node agent. However, the node agent has
not yet been materialized on a target server machine. This is sometimes called offline
node agent creation.

We can also create a node agent using the asadmin CLI. For example, to physically create a node agent, we use the following command:

```
# cd $AS_INSTALL/bin
# ./asadmin create-node-agent -H <admin-host> <node-agent-name>
```

This command must be executed on any server that will host server instances. Creating a node agent using the asadmin CLI is sometimes called online deployment, because this command will create a materialized agent. In the above command, the option -H <admin-host> indicates the DAS host name. This parameter is necessary because each node agent must know which DAS it should communicate with.

 A node agent must be materialized before it can be started. Due to this, if we have created a node agent using the Admin Console, we still need to use the asadmin CLI to create one that has the same name as the place holder name specified in the Admin Console.

After creating the node agent, we can start it by using the start-node-agent command of the asadmin CLI on the machine where the node agent is defined, for example:

```
# cd $AS_INSTALL/bin
# ./asadmin start-node-agent osdev
```

The next step is to define a cluster, create several server instances, and add the server instances to the cluster.

Creating clusters

We can create a cluster using either the Admin Console or the asadmin CLI's create-cluster command. To use the Admin Console, complete the following steps:

1. Log on to the Admin Console.
2. Click **Clusters** in the navigation panel.
3. Click **New** in the content panel.
4. Enter appropriate information, as shown in the following screenshot, and click **OK**.

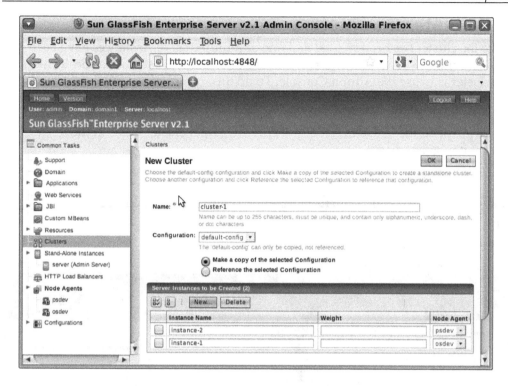

The parameters shown in the above screenshot are explained as follows:

- Name: Each cluster must have a unique name.

- Configuration: For GlassFish running in the cluster or enterprise profile, the GlassFish Server provides two configuration templates. The `server-config` template defines the default configuration data for the DAS server. The `default-config` is used to provide the same for other server instances or clusters. Typically, we can select `default-config` and make a copy of the selected configuration. For clusters, GlassFish will make a copy of the `default-config`, and save it under the name `<cluster-name>-config`.

- Server instances to be clustered: All the server instances of a cluster must be managed through node agents. Therefore, for each server instance we want to add to the cluster, we need to specify a name and associate it with a defined node agent.

 We can create server instances of a cluster using the offline node agent place holders. Also, server instances can be created or deleted after the cluster has been created.

Clusters can be also created using the `create-cluster` command of the `asadmin` CLI.

Administering clusters

Once the cluster has been created and one or multiple server instances have been added to the cluster, we can start administering it. The easiest way to administer the cluster is to use the Admin Console. To do this, complete the following steps:

1. Log on to the Admin Console.
2. Expand the **Clusters** node, and click the target cluster name in the navigation panel.

The following screenshot shows the cluster administration interface.

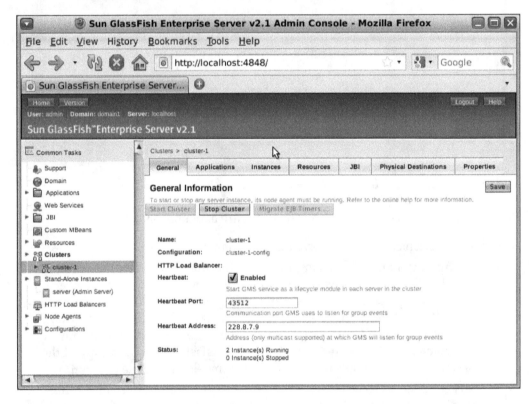

The **General** tab of the cluster management page allows us to do the following:

*   Start and stop the server instances of the cluster.
*   Enable the **Group Management Service (GMS)** for in-memory replication. We will discuss GMS in more detail later in this chapter.
*   Configure EJB timer migration.

The **Applications** tab allows us to track applications deployed to the cluster, and it also allows us to enable, disable, deploy, and remove applications. In addition, when we use a load balancer to distribute the processing across multiple server instances of the cluster, we can enable or display one of the cluster-deployed applications for load balancing. The **Resources** tab allows us to track the Java EE resources used in our environment. It also allows us to deploy new resources to GlassFish. Other tabs of the cluster management page are actually very similar to the tabs for the Application Server node for GlassFish running in the developer profile. For example, if we want to create a new JDBC resource, we can click the **Resources** tab, and it will allow us to create the desired JDBC resource. The **Physical Destinations** tab tracks the MQ destinations created for the new cluster.

Creating server instances for the cluster

The **Instances** tab of the cluster configuration page allows us to manage the server instances defined for the cluster. It also allows us to create new server instances for the cluster. The `create-instance` command of the `asadmin` CLI utility can perform the same functionality.

We can also configure each server instance's weight in the cluster. As we will see later in this chapter, the weight value will affect how a load balancer distributes load among the server instances.

Now that we have created node agents, clusters, and server instances, let's examine another piece of the puzzle—the load balancer.

Configuring load balancers

For a cluster with multiple server instances, using a load balancer in front of the server instances not only simplifies the client's view of the system through a single address, but also improves the overall system's reliability. If one server fails, the load balancer can detect the failure and distribute the load to other live server instances. In this section, we will discuss the load balancer support in GlassFish, and how to configure it.

GlassFish can work with a variety of load balancers, both hardware and software based. For example, the GlassFish project maintains and releases a load balancer plug-in, which works with Apache, Sun Java System Web Server, and Microsoft IIS. The load balancer plug-in is freely downloadable at `http://download.java.net/javaee5/external/<os>/aslb/jars`, where `<os>` indicates the operating system on which the web server is running.

Also, GlassFish can be load balanced by Apache using mod_jk. However, the mod_jk based load balancing is not officially supported in GlassFish 2. In this chapter, we will focus on the GlassFish load balancer plugin.

 The mod_jk based load balancing will be supported in GlassFish 3.

The GlassFish load balancer plug-in accepts HTTP and HTTPS requests and forwards them to one of GlassFish instances in the cluster. It uses a health checker to detect server instance status. If a server instance fails, requests are redirected to existing, available machines. Once a failed server instance comes back online, the load balancer can also recognize when a failed instance has recovered and redistributed the load accordingly.

Like most load balancer solutions for web applications, the GlassFish load balancer plugin implements session affinity or sticky session. On the first request from a client, a new session is established on the server instance node that is processing the request. The load balancer routes all subsequent requests for this session to that particular instance.

The load balancer plugin configuration actually involves two steps. First, we need to configure the web server to enable the load balancer; we then need to configure the GlassFish Server to specify how the load balancer should be configured for a cluster, or an application in a cluster.

In the following section, let's discuss how to configure the Apache web server for the load balancer plugin.

Configuring the load balancer plug-in for Apache web server

The Apache web server is the most popular web server. Its modular architecture makes it easy to extend for additional functionality. The GlassFish load balancer plugin for Apache is configured as an additional module. In this section, we discuss how to configure this module.

In this section, we discuss the configuration of the load balancer plug-in for the default Apache server, version 2.2, with SSL enabled on port 443, installed on Solaris x86. The configuration process for other operating systems is very similar; the only difference is the directory structure of the Apache server. For more detailed information, you can refer to the *GlassFish High Availability Administration Guide*, located at http://docs.sun.com/app/docs/doc/821-0182.

Complete the following steps to configure the load balancer plug-in on the Apache web server:

1. Download the latest load-balancer plug-in from http://download.java.net/javaee5/external/<os>/aslb/jars. Extract the JAR file, and then extract the two ZIP files, SUNWaspx.zip and SUNWaslb.zip to a directory, $lbplug-in_root.

2. Copy the errorpages directory from $lbplug-in_root/lib/webserver-plug-in/<os>/apache2.2 to /usr/apache2/2.2/modules/errorpages. The errorpages directory contains the web pages used by the load balancer plug-in to render load balancer error messages.

3. Copy the two files, LBPlug-inDefault_root.res and LBPlug-inD_root.res from $lbplug-in_root/lib/webserver-plug-in/<os>/apache2.2 to the /usr/apache2/2.2/modules/resource directory.

4. Copy the three files, cert8.db, key3.db, and secmpd.db from $lbplug-in_root/lib/webserver-plug-in/<os>/apache2.2 to the /usr/apache2/2.2/sec_db_files directory.

5. Copy the file mod_load_balancer.so from $lbplug-in_root/lib/webserver-plug-in/<os>/apache2.2 to the /usr/apache2/2.2/libexec directory.

6. Copy the file loadbalancer.xml.example from $lbplug-in_root/lib/install/templates to the /etc/apache2/2.2/loadblancer.xml. The loadbalancer.xml file is the primary configuration file that defines the load balancer. We will discuss this file in the next section. At this moment, we can consider it as a place holder.

7. Copy the file `sun-loadbalancer_1_2.dtd` from `$lbplug-in_root/lib/dtds` to `/etc/apache2/2.2`.

8. Append the following elements to `/etc/apache2/2.2/conf.d/modules-32.load`:

   ```
   LoadModule apachelbplug-in_module libexec/mod_loadbalancer.so
   <IfModule apachelbplug-in_module>
   config-file /etc/apache2/2.2/loadbalancer.xml
   </IfModule>
   ```

9. Add the following definition of the `LD_LIBRARY_PATH` variable to `/etc/apache2/2.2/envvars`:

   ```
   LD_LIBRARY_PATH=/usr/lib/mps:$lbplug-in_root/lib:/usr/apache2/2.2/libexec:$LD_LIBRARY_PATH
   ```

10. Copy the `mpm.conf` file from the `/etc/apache2/2.2/envvars/samples-conf.d` directory to `/etc/apache2/2.2/envvars/conf.d`, and change the values of the `StartServers` and `MaxClients` variables in the file to 1. This change is necessary. Otherwise, every new session request will spawn a new Apache process and the load balancer plug-in will be initialized resulting in requests landing in the same instance.

11. Restart the Apache server.

Once we have applied these steps to the Apache web server, it is ready to work as a load balancer for our GlassFish cluster. As we discussed earlier, the essential configuration file for the load balancer plug-in is `loadbalancer.xml`. This file captures the essential information about the server instances being load balanced, and the load distribution configuration. This information is actually generated on the GlassFish Server, and then transferred to the web server. In the next section, let's discuss how we can configure the load balancer information on GlassFish.

Configuring GlassFish for load balancing

Once the web server has been configured, we can define a GlassFish load balancer configuration. This can be done using the Admin Console, or the `create-http-lb` command of the `asadmin` CLI utility. To create a load balancer configuration using the Admin Console, click the **HTTP Load Balancer** node in the navigational panel, and then click **New** in the content panel. The following screenshot shows the input form for creating a load balancer configuration.

The important input parameters for the load balancer configuration are explained as follows:

- Name: A unique name of the new load balancer configuration.

- All instances: Where all the server instances of the selected target will be load balanced.

- All applications: Whether all the applications deployed to the target will be load balanced.

- Device host and admin port: The load balancing device's server information. GlassFish can rely on this information to automatically push the new load balancer configuration information to the device.

For software load balancers, the device is the server that runs the load balancing software. The admin port is the port through which administration tasks can be performed on the load balancing device. The port must be SSL enabled. If the device requires authentication, you should configure the device to support client certificate authentication. The information is used purely for pushing the load balancer configuration. Therefore, if you have a different mechanism to transfer the information, the device host and admin port values are not important, even though they are necessary.

- Automatically apply changes: Whether GlassFish pushes the new load balancer configuration information immediately to the device.

- Targets: The clusters and server instances that will participate in the load balancing.

Once the load balancer configuration is created, we can modify the settings for the load balancer, including the following parameters:

- Response timeout: Time in seconds within which a server instance must return a response. If no response is received within the time period, the server is considered unhealthy. The default is 60.

- HTTPS routing: Whether HTTPS requests to the load balancer result in HTTPS or HTTP requests to the server instance. For more information, see Configuring HTTPS Routing.

- Reload pool interval: Interval between checks for changes to the load balancer configuration file `loadbalancer.xml`. When the check detects changes, the configuration file is reloaded. A value of 0 disables reloading.

- Monitoring: Whether monitoring is enabled for the load balancer.

- Route cookie: Whether to use cookie to store the session routing information. Name of the cookie the load balancer plug-in uses to record the route information.

- Target: Target for the load balancer configuration. If you specify a target, it is the same as adding a reference to it. Targets can be clusters or stand-alone instances.

In addition, we can configure the load balancing algorithm, and the health checker of the load balance plug-in. By default, the load balancer uses simple round-robin mechanism to distribute the load across server instances. The load balancer plug-in also supports a weighted round robin algorithm; it allows us to favor certain instances based on their relative weights. If neither algorithm satisfies the requirement, we can develop a custom algorithm.

By default, the health checker of the load balancer plugin uses a specified URL to check all unhealthy GlassFish instances, and determines if they have returned to the healthy state. If the health checker finds that an unhealthy instance has become healthy, that instance is added to the list of healthy instances, and the load balancer will distribute load to it.

To configure the health checker, click the **Target** tab of the load balancer configuration form, and click the **Edit Health Check** link of a specific target.

The load balancing algorithm and health checker configuration form is shown in the following screenshot.

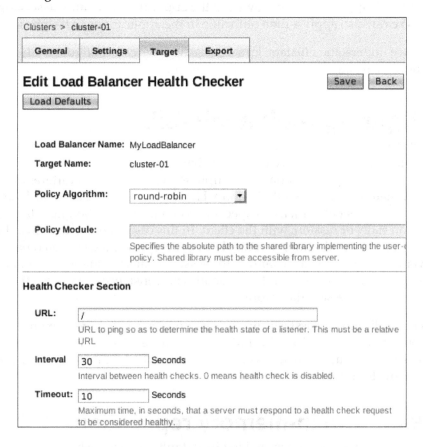

If we click the **Export** tab in the load balancer editing form, we get the options to either export the load balancer configuration as `loadbalancer.xml` file. This file can be copied to the load balancer host, which effectively updates the load balancer information. We can also click **Apply Changes Now** to push the configuration, provided that the load balancer device is configured appropriately.

Disabling (Quiescing) targets and applications

In a production environment, when we need to shut down a target, such as a server instance or cluster, we would like the target to shut down gracefully, that is, it stops accepting new requests and it keeps working until it has finished processing all the existing requests. This mechanism is called quiescing. The load balancer plug-in supports quiescing. In addition, it allows us to specify a timeout. If the target is still processing some existing request when the timeout limit is reached, the target will be shut down.

Similarly, in GlassFish, we can quiesce an application. For example, before we undeploy a web application, we may want the application to complete serving requests. We can also apply a time out value to the applications to be quiesced.

Now that we understand clusters, let's discuss how we can configure a GlassFish cluster for high availability in the following section.

Configuring high availability

Availability is typically measured in the form of system down time. The single most important mechanism to achieve high availability (HA) is through redundancy and replication. For example, by running multiple server instances on different hardware, we are eliminating a single point of failure. However, in many cases, hardware redundancy alone is not sufficient, especially when the application maintains a conversation state, or session, with the client. In this case, in order to deliver high availability for the application, we must be able to replicate the session data so that in the event of a server instance failure, the session state information maintained in that server instance is not lost, and a different server instance can restore the session from the replicated session data store.

For session replication, GlassFish supports two options, using the in-memory replication, and using the **High Availability Database** (**HADB**) for more reliable state persistence. In the following section, we discuss both of these options, and show you how to configure them.

Working with in-memory replication

In-memory session replication is enabled by default for GlassFish running in the cluster profile. It provides a light-weight failover mechanism that is high performance, and easy to configure. The high-level architecture of in-memory replication is illustrated in the following figure.

In this figure, a cluster of four server instances are running on two different server hosts. Each server instance not only maintains a data store for sessions established on itself, it also maintains a replicated data store of one of the server instance in the cluster. For example, the session store of server instance 1 is replicated in server instance 2, whose session store is replicated in server instance 3, and so on. Effectively, the server instances form a replication ring.

 In order to take advantage of in-memory session replication, make sure all the server instances of a cluster belong to the same subnet.

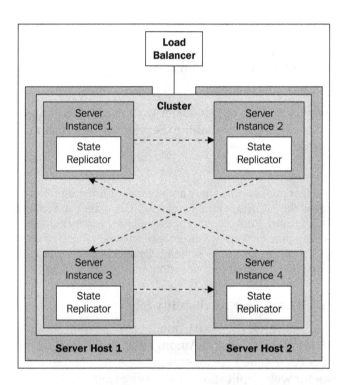

As we can see, in the normal state, every session is maintained by one server instance, and replicated in another server instance. If server instance 1 fails, a session originally established on server instance 1 can be failed over to server instance 2 without interruption.

If two adjacent server instances in the ring fail at the same time, some session state information will be lost. For example, if both server instance 1 and 2 fail, those sessions established on instance 1 will be lost. Due to this, in-memory replication may not be as reliable as more sophisticated mechanisms. However, if server instances are running on different physical hardware, the likelihood of both server instances failing can be greatly reduced.

In addition, in-memory replication provides very high performance, and its configuration is extremely simple. Due to this, in practice, unless the system availability requirement is very high, we strongly recommend you use in-memory replication.

Now, let's see how easy it is to configure in-memory replication.

Configuring in-memory replication

Configuring in-memory replication is very straightforward. We can configure it using the Admin Console as follows:

1. Log on to the Admin Console, expand the **Configurations** node, and then expand the cluster's configuration node.

2. Click **Availability Service**.

   The Availability Service of the cluster is shown in the Admin Console. You should see that the Availability Service for the cluster is enabled, which is the default value.

> Note that on the form, there are several additional properties, such as the MQ Store Pool Name and HA Store Name and so on. The MQ Store Pool Name property allows us to provide a JDBC resource as a message persistence mechanism (the default persistence mode for Open MQ is filesystem). Other HA related properties are related to the HADB configuration.

3. Click the **Web Container Availability** tab.

   Now we can configure the Web Container for session replication, as shown in the following figure. Among others, the most important parameter is **Persistent Type**. It specifies the session persistence mechanism for web applications that have availability enabled. For the cluster profile of GlassFish, the default value is `replicated`, meaning the web container session state is replicated in-memory.

   For a more detailed description of other parameters, you can refer to the *GlassFish High Availability Guide*.

4. Click the **EJB Container Availability** tab, and we can configure the availability service for stateful session beans. The parameters for EJB container's availability are similar to those for web container availability.

5. Click the **JMS Availability** tab, and we can configure the Open MQ based JMS service for high availability. We can specify a JDBC resource as the JMS message persistence mechanism (The default message persistence for Open MQ is done using the filesystem).

OpenMQ supports Message Broker clusters that can be deployed as an enterprise-level, high performance, and highly available message backbone. GlassFish's JMS resources can take full advantage of a clustered Open MQ installation. Discussing Open MQ Broker clustering is out of scope of this book. You can refer to the Open MQ documentation and the *GlassFish High Availability Administration Guide* for more information.

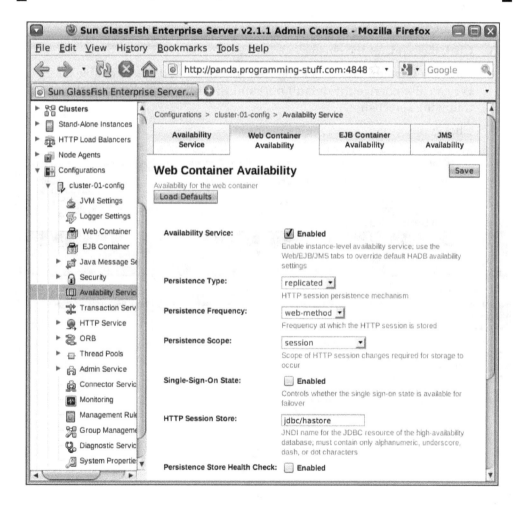

Configuring the Group Member Service (GMS)

The in-memory state replication in GlassFish relies on the Group Management Service (GMS) for keeping track of the server instance status. GMS is based on the open source project Shoal (`https://shoal.dev.java.net`). It uses an event driven mechanism to track the group membership. For example, when a server instance of a cluster fails, GMS uses an event to notify the cluster about the state change, and all other server instances will reform a replication ring (this is called a reshape).

By default, GMS is enabled for a cluster. We can disable/enable it using the Admin Console by following these steps:

1. Log on to the Admin Console.
2. Click **Clusters** in the navigation pane.
3. Click the name of the cluster.
4. Click the **General** tab. Check the **Heartbeat Enabled** box to enable GMS. We can also change the default port and IP address, as shown in the following screenshot.
5. Click **Save**.

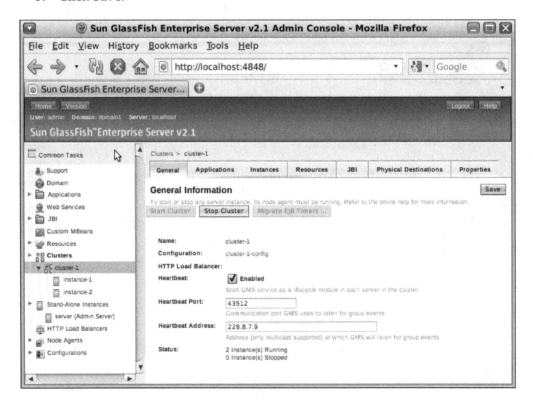

Once GMS is enabled for the cluster, the cluster's configuration will contain the parameters for the Group Management Services, and we can change these settings to suit our need. To configure GMS in the Admin Console, complete the following steps:

1. Log on to the Admin Console.

2. Expand the **Configurations** node in the navigation pane, and then expand the configuration for the cluster.

3. Click **Group Management Service**. The Group Management Service parameters should be displayed in the content pane, as shown in the following screenshot.

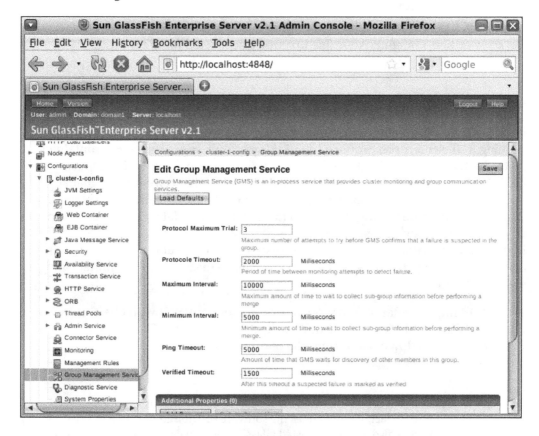

4. Set the parameters to appropriate values, and click **Save**.

The configurable parameters for GMS are as follows:

- **Protocol Maximum Trial**: Maximum number of attempts before GMS confirms that a failure is suspected in the group

- **Protocol Timeout**: Period of time between monitoring attempts to detect Failure

- **Maximum Interval**: Maximum amount of time to wait to collect sub-group information before performing a merge

- **Minimum Interval**: Minimum amount of time to wait to collect sub-group information before performing a merge

- **Ping Timeout**: Amount of time that GMS waits for discovery of other members in this group

- **Verified Timeout**: After this timeout, a suspected failure is marked as verified

HADB-based session failover

HADB-based session persistence is another option supported for GlassFish Server running in the enterprise profile. Using this approach, session state is maintained by the high availability database. Compared to the in-memory session replication, the HADB approach is definitely heavy weight. Not only do we need to manage the GlassFish cluster, we also need to configure the HADB. In addition, there is definitely an overhead using the HADB to persist session data. However, the HADB-based session persistence is a proven technology that can produce very high system availability. Due to this, for systems with availability being the number one priority, using HADB as the session persistence mechanism is definitely an excellent choice.

The HADB implementation is not open source, therefore, you won't be able to download the GlassFish Server with HADB support from the GlassFish website. However, you can download it from the Sun download site `http://www.sun.com/software/products/appsrvr`.

 This version of the GlassFish Server can be considered as the "enterprise edition". In fact, not only does the software distribution include the HADB support, it also includes a tested GlassFish load balancer plug-in, and it is also bundled with several additional resources, such as JDBC drivers.

Installing the GlassFish Server with HADB software is relatively easy, as its graphical installer is very simple. The only caveat is that when you install the software, you will be asked if you want to install the load balancer plug-in. In order to install the load balancer plug-in, a supported web server must be pre-installed on the system. If you don't have a supported web server installed, you can simply skip it. As we have seen earlier in this chapter, we can always manually configure the load balancer later.

Configuring HADB enabled clusters is much more involved than configuring clusters using in-memory session replication. Refer to the *GlassFish High Availability Administration Guide*.

Summary

In this chapter, we showed you how to configure clusters and high availability for GlassFish. We also showed you how to use a load balancer to distribute the load across multiple server instances. At this point, you should have a clear understanding of GlassFish clusters and the high availability configuration options.

In the next chapter, we will discuss the tuning and troubleshooting part of administering the GlassFish Server.

10
Troubleshooting and Tuning GlassFish

In this chapter, we will discuss one of the more difficult areas of administering any server environment, including GlassFish: troubleshooting and performance tuning. Due to the inherent complexity of this topic, instead of trying to cover too much briefly, we try to focus on several practical tools that can make our job of maintaining and tuning GlassFish easier. The goal of this chapter is to help you gain a high level of understanding on what is involved when we troubleshoot and tune GlassFish, and then help you get familiar with the tools. Along the way, we will also point you to appropriate resources for an in-depth coverage of specific topics.

Troubleshooting the GlassFish environment

Like any other server environment, sometimes, the GlassFish Server environment can go wrong. Errors could come in many different forms. For example, the GlassFish Server may not be able to start if there is port number conflict; or an application may exhibit strange behavior when the server is under heavy load. The official GlassFish troubleshooting guide (`http://docs.sun.com/app/docs/doc/820-4339`) maintains a list of commonly occurred problems, and also provides the solution to them. We strongly recommend that you get familiar with this document.

In our experience, the most difficult issues occur in applications and their configuration. In other words, the GlassFish Server is in a running state, but the deployed applications are not producing desired results. What makes the matter more difficult is that many application or configuration related errors do not surface until they are running under some unexpected circumstances, such as very heavy server load. For these types of errors, it is difficult to provide one solution that works all the time.

However, we are not completely helpless. As we will see in the following sections, there are many tools that can notify us on the situation, capture the error, and help us find a resolution. For example, all the monitoring tools we discussed in Chapter 8, Monitoring GlassFish can be very helpful because they produce detailed monitoring information. In this chapter, we introduce several additional tools that also help us discover and resolve issues in GlassFish.

Using the diagnostic service

The GlassFish diagnostic service provides a convenient mechanism to create a diagnostics report that captures a lot of critical information about the GlassFish Server. This allows the GlassFish administrator to create a complete and unambiguous archive, and send it to the GlassFish supporting group for supporting services.

The diagnostics report is generated as a JAR file that includes the following information: system information, all the monitor-able attribute values, application server configuration files, all the deployed applications, and the server log files. To create a diagnostic report, complete the following steps:

1. Log on to the GlassFish Server Admin Console.
2. Click the **Application Server** node in the **Navigation Panel**, and select the **Diagnostics** tab in the main content panel.

The Admin Console displays a form that collects additional information about the content of the diagnostics report, such as the date range of the server log files, as shown in the following screenshot.

 If the Application server is running in the cluster or enterprise profile, then the diagnostics service is accessible by clicking the **Domain** node in the navigation service. In addition, if the domain has node agents, clusters, and additional server instances configured, we can choose whether the diagnostics report is for the entire domain: a cluster, a server instance, or a node agent.

3. Fill out the form with appropriate information, and click **Generate Report**. Click **OK** to accept the warning about confidential information being captured in the report.

 We can create password aliases to avoid capturing confidential information, particularly passwords, in the report. Please refer to Chapter 7, *Securing GlassFish*, on how to do this.

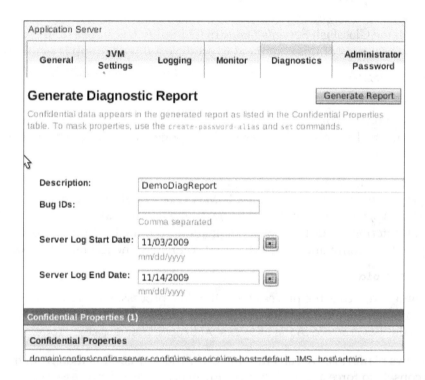

Once the diagnostics report is created, it is stored as a time stamped JAR file in the `$AS_INSTALL/domains/domain1/diagnostic-reports` directory. You can extract this JAR file to inspect the diagnostic report.

Finally, the diagnostic report can also be generated with the `generate-diagnostics-report` command of the `asadmin` CLI utility.

Working with thread dumps

When we troubleshoot Java, especially server-side Java applications, it is very common that we need to analyze the JVM's thread dump to discover issues such as thread deadlocks. In this section, we discuss how to create a thread dump, and how to analyze the thread dump.

Generating thread dumps

There are several different ways to generate the thread dump of the GlassFish Server. First, the GlassFish Server's `asadmin` CLI utility has a `generate-jvm-report` command. The syntax of this command to produce a thread dump is as follows:

```
# cd $AS_INSTALL/bin
# ./asadmin generate-jvm-report --type=thread
```

Notice the option `--type=thread`, because the `generate-jvm-report` command can also generate the reports for other JVM components such as the heap memory, and classes loaded.

Next, as long as the JVM is not running with the option `-Xrs` (reduce system signals usage), generating a thread dump for a JVM is very straight forward. On UNIX or Linux platforms, we can simply send a `-QUIT` signal to the JMV process. This can be done by entering the `CRTL-\` key combination from the JVM process console, or running the `kill` command from a different command line terminal, for example:

```
# kill -QUIT pid
```

In this command, `pid` is the process ID of the JMV process. For example, when we run this command against the GlassFish Server process, the thread dump will be written to the `jvm.log` file in the `$AS_INSTALL/domains/domain1/logs`.

On Windows platforms, we can enter the *Ctrl-Break* key combination from the JVM process console to force a thread dump. However, for server processes such as GlassFish that run in background without a live console, Windows does not provide a built-in tool to force a thread dump.

A third method to generate a thread dump is to take advantage of the tools in the JDK software. Starting from Java SE 5, the JDK software distribution is bundled with several very useful tools. One of these tools is `jstack`. The `jstack` command prints the current JVM's stack trace, which provides a readable thread dump of the JVM. The syntax of the `jstack` tool is very simple, as it simply provides the process ID of the JVM:

```
# jstack pid > jstacl.tdump
```

Typically, we redirect the `jstack` tool into a file as shown in the command, because we can analyze the data later.

Finally, the VisualVM tool that we discussed in Chapter 8 can also be used to generate a thread dump. To do this, just connect to the JVM process, select the **Threads** tab, and click the **Thread Dump** button, as shown in the following screenshot:

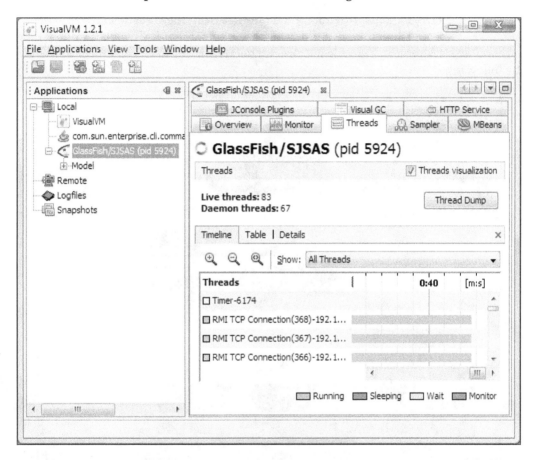

The thread dump generated using the `jstack` and VisualVM tools are in the same format, all the other tools mentioned earlier generate the thread dump in slightly different formats.

Once we have generated the thread dump, we can use a tool to analyze it. In the next section, we discuss how to use the open source thread dump analysis tool, TDA (`https://tda.dev.java.net`) to do this.

Analyzing thread dumps using TDA

The TDA tool works with thread dumps generated by `jstack` or Visual VM. It can
run either as a standalone component, or as a plugin for the VisualVM tool. On this
section, we discuss how to use the TDA standalone tool. For information on adding
it to Visual VM, you can refer to the VisualVM documentation.

To install the TDA tool, just download the binaries from the website and extract the
ZIP file to a specific directory. After this, simply navigate to the installation directory,
and double click the `tda.jar` file to start it. The TDA tool's user interface is shown in
the following screenshot:

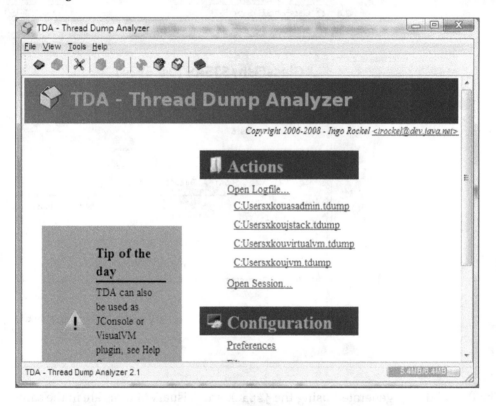

The TDA tool allows us to load any text file that includes a thread dump. For
example, to load the dump file produced by the `jstack` command, we can select
Load from the **File** menu and navigate to the location of the thread dump file.

Once the thread dump is loaded, the TDA tool displays the thread information in an intuitive manner, as shown in the following screenshot:

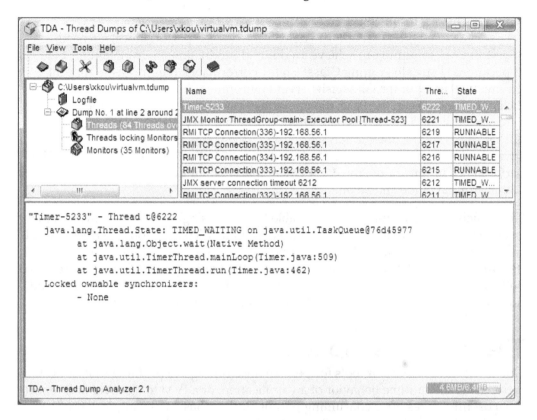

As we can see in the previous screenshot, the TDA tool shows all the thread's states, the monitors that are maintained in the JVM, and how multiple threads are waiting for the same monitor. This data can be highly effective for finding thread-related issues, such as deadlock. We strongly recommend you to spend time getting familiar with this tool.

In the next section, we discuss the tuning aspect of GlassFish, and introduce several more tools that help us do the job.

Tuning GlassFish Server for performance

The GlassFish Server is capable of delivering very high performance, as shown in the benchmark results (`http://www.spec.org/jAppServer2004/results/jAppServer2004.html`). In order to deliver the desired performance, we need to perform careful tuning to achieve an optimal production environment for our applications. Typically, tuning GlassFish for performance requires us to tune all the involved areas of the GlassFish Server environment including any applications, the application server, the JVM, the operating system, and the underlying hardware system. This makes performance tuning a very diverse topic. The official GlassFish documentation set (`http://docs.sun.com/app/docs/prod/gf.entsvr.v21`) contains the multiple documents dedicated to tuning, such as the performance tuning guide, the deployment planning guide, and the high availability administration guide and so on.

Given such a diverse topic, it is impossible to write a single chapter to cover all the issues. Due to this, we took a more focused approach. This section describes several readily available tools that allow us to understand the nature of our application and its hosting GlassFish Server environment, and then quickly identify the performance bottleneck or some runtime issues. First, we will discuss the NetBeans profiler, and how we can use it to profile our applications for performance characteristics.

The NetBeans profiler

One of the most important tools for performance tuning is a profiling tool. A profiler can analyze the runtime behavior of an application, or a JVM to discover and report the most time or resource consuming part of applications. For example, a profiler can tell us the most frequently called methods in an application, and the most time consuming operations. The information should be considered as the definitive information source for performance tuning. Without a profiler, we may end up spending a lot of efforts tuning one part of the system that is barely touched.

There are many profiling products. One of them, the NetBeans profiler (`http://profiler.netbeans.org`) has been under active development recently. As an open source profiler that is freely available, the NetBeans profiler offers a large set of excellent features. In this section, let's discuss how to use it to profile the GlassFish Server runtime, including deployed applications.

In the following section, we show you how to use the NetBeans profiler to profile a GlassFish Server instance.

Using the NetBeans profiler

In order to use the NetBeans profile, we need to download and install the NetBeans IDE (`http://netbeans.org`). Once this is done, let's go through the following steps to profile a remote GlassFish Server instance running on a different host:

1. Start the NetBeans IDE.

2. From the **Profile** menu, select **Attach Profiler**. We should see a dialog window pop up, as shown in the following screenshot.

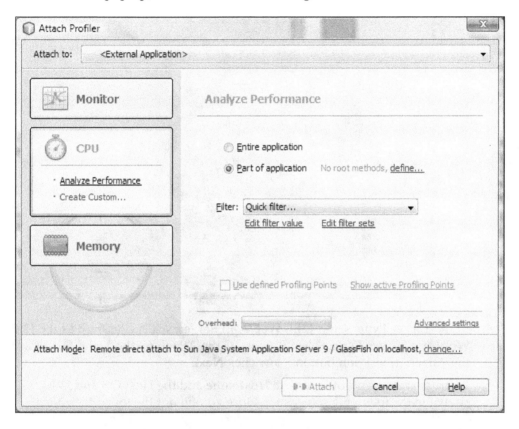

3. Click **change...** in the dialog to change the remote GlassFish Server information. We should see the **Select Target Type** dialog appear, as shown in the following screenshot.

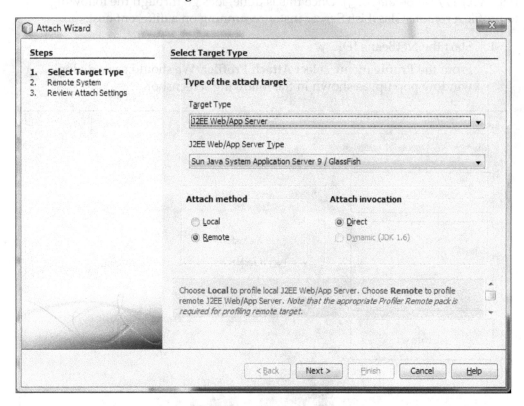

4. In the **Target Type**, select **J2EE Web/App Server**; select GlassFish as the **J2EE Web/App Server Type**. Select **Remote** as the **Attach method**, and **Direct** as the **Attach invocation** button. Now click **Next**.

5. In the next step, enter the remote **Hostname** and the **Host OS and JVM**, as shown in the following screenshot. Once you fill out the form, click **Next**.

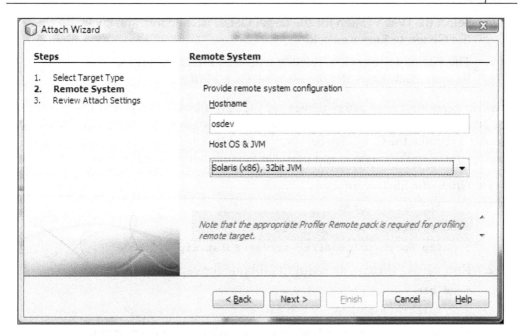

6. In the following review dialog screen, click **Next**. The manual dialog appears, as shown in the following screenshot.

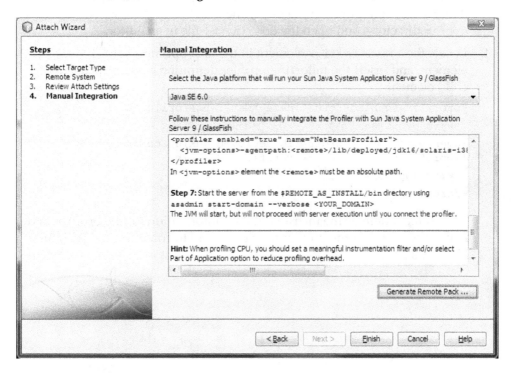

7. Select the JVM version for the target GlassFish version, and click the **Generate Remote Pack**.

8. The **File** dialog appears. Select the desired directory, and save the **Remote Pack**. Once the file is saved, click **Finish**.

This will generate a `profiler-server-$plat.zip` file, where `$plat` indicates the platform on which the GlassFish Server is running, such as `solx86` (Solaris x86). In order to profile the GlassFish Server, we need to copy this file to the target host running the GlassFish Server, and perform the following configuration:

1. Unzip the file to a directory.

```
# mkdir $profiler-dir
# cd $profiler-dir
# unzip $path-to/profiler-server-$plat.zip
```

2. Run the `calibrate.sh` script to calibrate the capability of the host.

```
# cd bin
# ./calibrate.sh
```

The calibration command calculates the adjustment necessary for the profiling measurement to make it more accurate.

3. Shut down the GlassFish Server if it is running. Back up a copy of the `domain.xml` configuration file under the `$AS_INSTALL/domains/domain1/config` directory, and open the `domain.xml` file in an editor.

4. Locate the `<java-config>` element in the appropriate `<server-config>` element, and insert the following profiler definition element as its first child element:

```
<profiler enabled="true" name="NetBeansProfiler">
  <jvm-options>
-agentpath:$profilerdir/lib/deployed/jdk16/$os-arch/
libprofilerinterface.so=$rprofiler-dir/lib,5140
  </jvm-options>
</profiler>
```

This element defines the instrumentation information for the profiler, and it also specifies that the profiler uses port `5140` to communicate with the NetBeans profiler.

The asadmin CLI has a command create-profiler. It creates the profiler element as shown in the previous snippet. However, due to the difference among profiler products, you still need to provide more detailed information about it, such as the <jvm-option> element shown previously.

5. Restart GlassFish with the verbose option:

```
# cd SAS_INSTALL/bin
# ./asadmin start-domain -verbose
```

6. The –verbose option displays the GlassFish Server runtime status in the startup terminal.

7. From the NetBeans IDE, select **Attach Profiler...** from the **Profiler** menu.

8. In the **Attach a Profiler** dialog, you can select one of the options, **Monitor**, **CPU | New CPU Analysis**, or **Memory**, and then click the **Attach** button.

9. Once the NetBeans Profiler is attached to the GlassFish Server, the profiler view appears in the NetBeans IDE, as shown in the following screenshot:

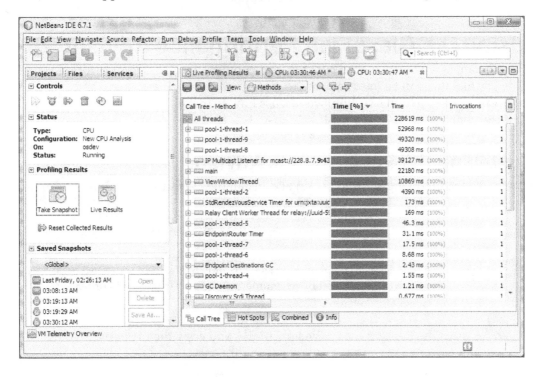

The NetBeans profiler allows you to view the live results, and it also allows us to take snapshots, save them, and compare with other snapshots. This feature is helpful because it allows us to tune the application, run performance testing, and compare the results of different tuning options.

10. When you decide to stop profiling the GlassFish Server, select **Detach Profiler** from the profiler menu.

One thing to note is that when the profiler is detached, the GlassFish Server will shutdown. Once you decide that you no longer need to profile the GlassFish Server, you can either delete the profiler, or set the enabled property to `false` in the profiler element. After this modification, you can start the GlassFish Server.

The freely available NetBeans profiler provides a good starting point for gathering the performance characteristics of applications. The profiling information is essential for finding the performance bottleneck of the application so that we can make necessary modifications.

In the next section, we will discuss the performance advisor tool that Sun has made available for its customers with commercial support.

Using the GlassFish Performance Advisor

For customers with commercial support, Sun provides the GlassFish Performance Advisor tool that can be used to provide performance tuning assistance and performance alert. In this section, we discuss how to install and use the Performance Advisor tool.

Installing the Performance Advisor

Complete the following steps to obtain and install the Performance Advisor:

1. Download the Performance Advisor software, `140751-01.zip` from `http://www.sun.com/software/products/appsrvr/get_it.jsp`.

 This URL leads to the SunSolve website, `http://sunsolve.sun.com`. You need to log on, and have commercial support from Sun in order to download the software.

2. Extract the Performance Advisor ZIP file, and copy the file `performance-advisor.jar` to the `$AS_INSTALL/lib` directory.

3. Restart the GlassFish Server.

4. Once GlassFish restarts, open a browser, and log on to the Admin Console.

5. The **Performance Advisor** appears in the Admin Console as a top-level node, as shown in the following screenshot.

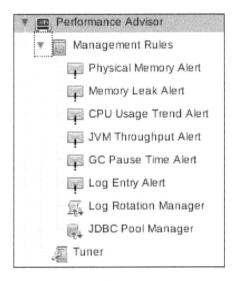

As we can see, the Performance Advisor contains two components— a set of predefined management rules and a performance tuner. In the following sections, we describe the usage of each component.

Using Performance Advisor management rules

Most of the predefined management rules in the Performance Advisor allow us to define alerts for common performance related issues, such as memory and CPU usage. Two of the management rules, the **Log Rotation Manager** and the **JDBC Pool Manager** also allow us to further control the logging system and the JDBC connection pools. For example, the JDBC Pool Manager allows us to further manage the maximum size of the JDBC connection pools. To configure this, complete the following steps:

1. Click the **JDBC Pool Manager** node in the Admin Console.

2. Click **Add**. The **JDBC Connection Pool Manager** configuration is shown in the following screenshot.

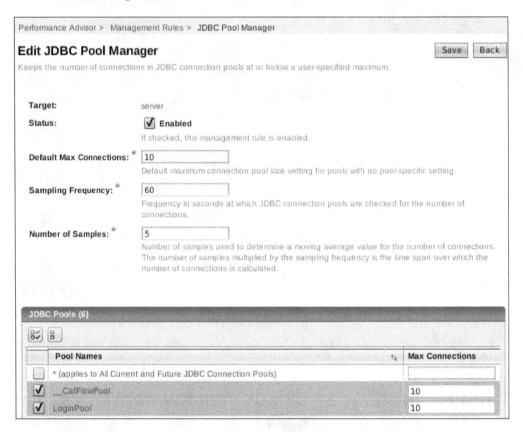

In this screenshot, the **Max Connections** property of each connection pool specifies the maximum number of connections each pool can maintain, and the **Default Max Connection** property sets the default value for connection pools that do not have Max Connections explicitly set.

3. Click **Save** to enable the management rule.

The maximum number of connections in the JDBC Pool Manager will override the maximum pool size value defined in each JDBC connection pool. This feature is useful for managing connections in deployment environments where multiple connection pools are connected to the same database. By having the management rule as an extra safeguard, we can better manage the total number of the connections to a database without having to manually change each connection pool's setting.

Configuring alert management rules is also quite simple. For example, to monitor the physical memory, simply add a **Physical Memory Alert** rule, and specify the free memory threshold that will trigger an alert, and select whether we want to enable e-mail notification, and click **Save**.

In order to enable e-mail notification, we must configure a JavaMail resource on GlassFish.

Using the Performance Advisor tuner

The Performance Advisor tuner checks the environment of the running GlassFish Server, collects the necessary configuration data, runs a static analysis based on Sun's application server tuning experience, and provides the recommended settings that should be applied to the server.

When we click the **Tuner** node in the Admin Console, the tuner wizard is displayed, as shown in the following screenshot.

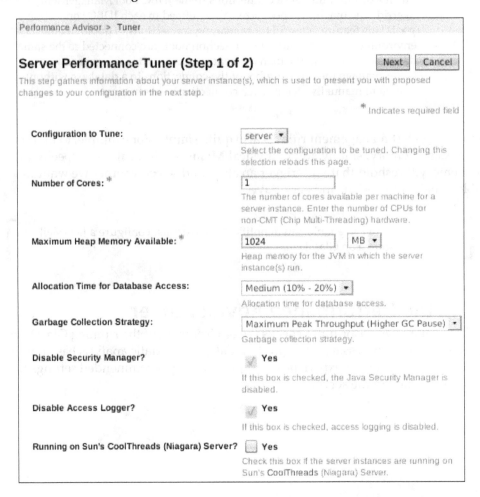

The performance advisor tuner relies on the properties shown in the previous screenshot to analyze the deployment environment, and create proposed configuration changes. For example, the **Configuration to Tune** property allows us to select which server instance or cluster to tune, and the **Allocation Time for Database Access** property allows us to specify the estimated amount of the time the GlassFish Server spends on accessing the backend database. For a complete description of these properties, you can refer to the *GlassFish Server Performance Advisor Installation and Quick Start Guide,* located at `http://docs.sun.com/app/docs/doc/820-7188`.

Once we have confirmed and made the necessary changes to the system settings, click **Next**. The Admin Console displays a table of proposed system setting variables and values, as shown in the following screenshot.

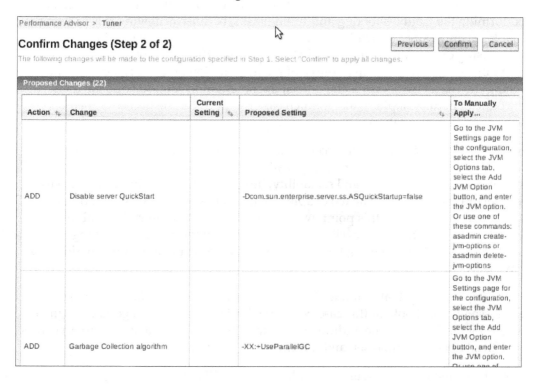

When we click **Confirm**, the proposed changes will be written to the domain.xml file, and we need to restart GlassFish to make the changes effective.

 The original domain.xml is backed up in the $AS_INSTALL/domain/ domain1/config/tuner directory.

The Performance Advisor may look like a simple tool, but it actually captures a lot of Sun's application tuning best practices, and it could yield excellent performance gains. You can find some white papers on GlassFish performance at http://java. sun.com/javaee/overview/whitepapers.

Summary

In this chapter, we discussed the troubleshooting and performance tuning aspects of the GlassFish Server. The intent of this chapter is not to provide a detailed recipe for performing the troubleshooting and tuning tasks, because achieving this in a single chapter is impossible. Instead, we treat this chapter as a practical starting point by focusing on several useful tools that help us identify and resolve some very common issues. The definitive source of the information on troubleshooting and tuning the GlassFish Server is the official documentation set. We hope the tools introduced in this chapter make it much easier to perform the tasks outlined in the official documentation.

In our opinion, GlassFish is an excellent Java EE application server that can go head-to-head against all the other application server products. It not only supports high performance and scalability, but also provides a simple yet effective administration interface. The ten chapters that you have just gone through have addressed most of it. At this point, we hope you are very comfortable with the GlassFish, and getting very excited about standing up the server, deploying applications, and maintaining the server environment with all the information you have learned.

In reality, it is likely that you might stumble upon some issues that were not addressed in this book. In this case, we hope this book has done a good enough job in getting familiar with the additional resources that are extremely valuable, such as its official documentation set, and the GlassFish community.

Good luck, and enjoy the journey of administering GlassFish.

11
Working with GlassFish 3

In this chapter, we will provide a brief introduction to the upcoming GlassFish version 3. First, we will discuss several main features of GlassFish 3. We will then discuss how to install GlassFish 3, followed by a discussion of the administrative infrastructure of GlassFish 3. Finally, we discuss how to deploy different types of applications to GlassFish 3.

 At the time of this writing, GlassFish 3 is still under development. Some of the information may be changed by the time GlassFish 3 is officially released. However, we hope this preview chapter provides you with enough information to get a head start with GlassFish 3.

Introducing GlassFish 3

Currently, GlassFish 3 is under active development, in parallel with the Java EE 6 standard. Like the previous versions, GlassFish 3 is being developed not only as a Java EE reference implementation, but also as an application server that delivers high performance and availability. In addition, a lot of new features were introduced into GlassFish 3 with the goal of making GlassFish more flexible, customizable, and to an extent, more "fun" to work with. In this section, we highlight several essential features of GlassFish 3.

New features of GlassFish 3

This section highlights several new features introduced in GlassFish 3. For a more complete description of the features of GlassFish 3, you can refer to the *GlassFish 3 Prelude Release Notes*, located at http://docs.sun.com/app/docs/doc/820-4494.

Supporting Java EE 6 profiles

Java EE 6 introduced the concept of technology profiles. Each profile specifies a set of specifications and APIs to facilitate the development of a particular type of Java EE applications. For example, the Java EE Web Profile defines a subset of the full Java EE profile, and the focus of the web profile is to provide a standard, light-weight server environment for Java EE web applications.

GlassFish 3 supports both the Java EE web profile and the full platform profile. In fact, the GlassFish 3 software has two distributions—the web profile and the full profile. Depending on the types of the applications we develop and deploy, we can choose whichever profile is more appropriate.

The Java EE profile support in GlassFish 3 is not quite the same as the usage profile in GlassFish 2. The usage profile in GlassFish 2 is focused on incrementally adding quality-of-service (QoS) features, such as clustering and persistent session fail over using HADB. The Java EE technology profile is focused on aligning Java EE specifications based on the type of applications. These two aspects are independent of each other. At this time, the focus of GlassFish 3 is on the technology profile. The clustering and fail over features will be made available in the GlassFish 3.1 release.

Modular design

Starting with GlassFish 3, the original monolithic GlassFish Server was split into OSGi based modules. The main goal of the modular design is to improve the overall flexibility and dynamic capability of GlassFish 3. The modular design allows us to install only the modules that are required for running the target application, and dynamically install additional modules depending on the need.

In GlassFish 3, the support for Java EE profiles is actually based on this modular design. The GlassFish 3 web distribution includes the modules for supporting web applications. We can dynamically upgrade the server installation to support the full Java EE platform profile; all it takes is to install additional modules.

This modular approach significantly reduces the GlassFish Server's footprint. For example, the baseline GlassFish 3 Prelude release is about 28MB only, and it provides all the capabilities for running web applications. Also, by including only the essential modules, GlassFish 3 can be embedded in an application to provide necessary services.

The modular design also improves the reusability of the modules. For example, other OSGi modules and/or Java Archive (JAR) modules can be added to the GlassFish Server to achieve additional capability. Through a standard **Service Provider Interface (SPI)**, this modular design also allows the GlassFish Server to be easily extended and customized.

Support for dynamic and scripting languages

Besides being the reference implementation of the Java EE, GlassFish 3 was implemented to provide better support for dynamic programming languages and frameworks, such as Ruby, Rails, Groovy and Grails. In GlassFish 2, we could assemble these applications as web applications and deploy them as WAR files. GlassFish 3 makes it much simpler to do this, because we can deploy a Rails application as it is without bundling it as a WAR file. GlassFish 3 also provides a container environment for these applications, which allows us to configure and manage the runtime environment of these applications.

In the next section, let's start installing GlassFish 3.

Installing GlassFish 3

As we have discussed earlier, the GlassFish 3 software has two distributions, the web profile, and the full Java EE profile. In this section, we discuss how to install the full Java EE profile distribution. The installation process for the web profile distribution is identical.

For each profile, the GlassFish community website makes two types of the GlassFish 3 binary distributions available: a platform independent ZIP file and an executable installer-based file for Microsoft Windows and UNIX-like operating systems (Solaris, Linux, Mac OSX, and so on). These two distributions contain the same GlassFish Server release and modules, except that the installer-based distribution contains a graphical installer, and it is also bundled with the standalone update tool that can be installed along with GlassFish.

To install the ZIP file distribution of GlassFish, complete the following steps:

1. Download the `latest-glassfish.zip` file from `http://download.java. net/glassfish/3/promoted`.

2. Unzip the `latest-glassfish.zip` file to a target directory, such as `C:\ Software\Sun` on Windows, or `/opt` on UNIX-like operation systems.

Unzipping the file creates a directory named `glassfish3`, which serves as the root directory of the server installation. You can rename this directory. This is helpful if you want to install several copies of GlassFish for testing purposes.

This is it. We have the ZIP file-based GlassFish distribution installed. Now, lets see how to install the installer-based distribution, and why it is sometimes worthwhile to follow the seemingly longer and more complicated process to install the installer-based distribution.

The installer-based GlassFish distribution is also very easy to install. For example, to install it on a UNIX-like platform, we can download the latest GlassFish 3 promoted build, `latest-glassfish-unix.sh` from `http://download.java.net/ glassfish/3/promoted`. Once downloaded, we can run the downloaded installer to start the installation as follows.

```
# chmod +x latest-glassfish-unix.sh
# ./latest-glassfish-unix.sh
```

More on the installer-based distribution

The installer-based GlassFish distribution supports several command-line options that can be used to customize the installation process for different purposes. For example, we can specify the levels and target directory of the installation logging. We can also run the installer in the dry run mode to collect installation input information in an answer file, and later use the answer file to install GlassFish on different server hosts. This feature is particularly useful if we need to manage the consistency of many GlassFish installations installed in an organization.

To check the available command-line options, simply do the following:

1. Open a command-line terminal, and change to the directory where the GlassFish installer is located.
2. Enter the following command:

   ```
   # ./latest-glassfish-unix.sh -h
   ```

On Windows, you should see a dialog window with the help information for the installer. On UNIX-like operating systems, the same information is displayed in the terminal window where the command was started.

A detailed description of these command-line options can be found in the GlassFish 3 documentation. The following procedure demonstrates how we can use the answer file and silent installation features of GlassFish:

1. From the command-line terminal, change to the directory including the downloaded installer file, and enter the following commands:

   ```
   # ./latest-glassfish-unix.sh -n glassfish-install.state
   ```

The -n option of the command runs the installer in the dry-run mode. The dry-run mode displays the same installer GUI screens to collect the input information, which is saved in the answer file specified in the command.

The following is a sample answer file, with user-provided information highlighted. This sample answer contains the same information that corresponds to the installation described before. The answer file is fairly self-explanatory. If you need a detailed description of the format of the answer file, you can refer to the GlassFish documentation.

```
#openInstaller Dry Run Answer File. This File can be used as input
to the openInstaller engine using the -a option.
#Thu Dec 11 21:56:58 EST 2008
RegistrationOptions.regoptions.CREATE_NEWACCT=CREATE_NEWACCT
glassfish.Administration.HTTP_PORT=8080
updatetool.Configuration.PROXY_PORT=
glassfish.Administration.ADMIN_PASSWORD=
RegistrationOptions.regoptions.SKIP_REGISTRATION=SKIP_REGISTRATION
updatetool.Configuration.PROXY_HOST=
SOAccountCreation.accountinfo.COUNTRY=
InstallHome.directory.INSTALL_HOME=/opt/glassfish-3
RegistrationOptions.regoptions.USE_EXISTINGACCT=USE_EXISTINGACCT
SOAccountCreation.accountinfo.FIRSTNAME=
glassfish.Administration.NON_ANONYMOUS=NON_ANONYMOUS
updatetool.Configuration.ALLOW_UPDATE_CHECK=false
glassfish.Administration.ADMIN_USER=
SOAccountCreation.accountinfo.PASSWORD=
SOAccountCreation.accountinfo.COMPANYNAME=
glassfish.Administration.ANONYMOUS=ANONYMOUS
SOAccountCreation.accountinfo.COUNTRY_DROP_DOWN=
SOAccountCreation.accountinfo.REENTERPASSWORD=
License.license.ACCEPT_LICENSE=0
RegistrationOptions.regoptions.USERNAME=
updatetool.Configuration.BOOTSTRAP_UPDATETOOL=false
SOAccountCreation.accountinfo.LASTNAME=
glassfish.Administration.ADMIN_PORT=4848
RegistrationOptions.regoptions.USERPASSWORD=
SOAccountCreation.accountinfo.EMAIL=
RegistrationOptions.regoptions.DUMMY_PROP=
```

2. After the dry-run mode, enter the following command to use the answer file to complete a silent installation of GlassFish:

```
# ./latest-glassfish-unix.sh -s -a glassfish-install.state
```

As you can see, if you need to install GlassFish on multiple server hosts, all you need to do is to create an answer file in the dry-run mode, and then use the answer file to drive the silent installation. Besides assuring the GlassFish Servers installed are all the same, this approach allows you to script the installation procedure. This can be a great feature for administrators.

Verifying the GlassFish installation

Once the installation is complete, we can verify the GlassFish installation with the following steps:

1. From a command-line terminal, enter the following commands to start the GlassFish Server:

```
# cd $AS_INSTALL/bin
```

```
# ./asadmin start-domain
```

The command line terminal should display the following information, indicating the GlassFish Server has started successfully:

```
Name of the domain started: [domain1] and its location: [/opt/
glassfish3/glassfish/domains/domain1].
```

```
Admin port for the domain: [4848].
```

2. Open a web browser and point it at http://localhost:8080.

Port 8080 is the default HTTP port used by GlassFish to serve normal web applications and content. If the installation was successful, you should see the default page of the GlassFish Server, as shown in the following screenshot.

3. Now try to access the GlassFish Admin Console by pointing the browser at `http://localhost:4848`.

   By default, port 4848 is used to serve the GlassFish Admin Console web application, which is bundled with the GlassFish Server distribution. However, in GlassFish 3, this application is not installed and loaded into the GlassFish Server runtime until it is requested. Because of this, the browser should briefly display a page that indicates that the Admin Console application is being loaded.

4. Once the Admin Console is loaded, its user interface is displayed in the browser window. If you followed the installation steps described earlier in the book, you should also see a dialog that asks you to register your GlassFish installation.

The installer-based GlassFish distribution also has a registration screen. If you registered back then, then you would not see this dialog here. For ZIP file-based GlassFish distribution, this dialog always appears.

5. Once you finish or cancel the registration, the Admin Console application is updated and displayed in the browser, as shown in the following screenshot:

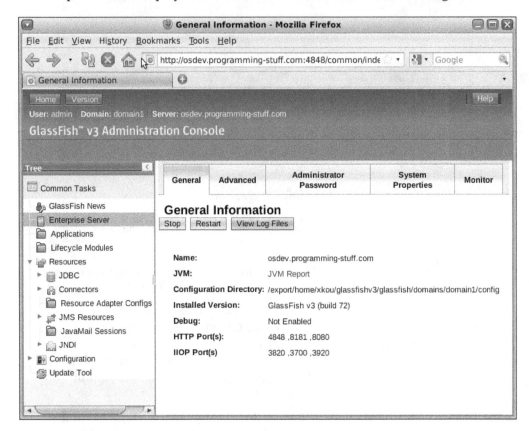

As you can see, it is very encouraging that the Admin Console of GlassFish 3 is very similar to that of GlassFish 2. In fact, you will see that other administration interfaces such as the asadmin CLI are also similar. Most of the administration topics we have discussed in the first ten chapters are very applicable for GlassFish 3 with minimal modification.

Working with the GlassFish update tool

GlassFish 3 adopted the **Image Packing System (IPS)** originally created for managing software package installation, removal, and update on the OpenSolaris operating system. The update tool of GlassFish provides a graphical user interface to the IPS system. In this section, we will explain the IPS package management mechanism for GlassFish, and discuss the update tool utility you can use to manage the GlassFish packages and components.

Introducing IPS

If you have used some popular Linux operating system distributions such as Ubuntu, you have probably installed and updated software packages using command-line utilities such as `apt-get`, or GUI based tools such as the Synaptic Package Manager. These package management utilities allow you to check what applications are installed, search some network repositories for new and updated applications, and download, and install them. Conceptually, the IPS mechanism is very similar to these package management systems. Originally developed for OpenSolaris, IPS has now evolved into an operating system and platform independent package system.

Within the GlassFish installation directory `$AS_INSTALL`, the hidden `.org.opensolaris,pkg` directory contains the meta-data of the packages in the current GlassFish installation. (On Windows, this directory is not hidden. Currently there is a bug open on this: `http://defect.opensolaris.org/bz/show_bug.cgi?id=853`). Essentially, the meta-data tracks the following information about the GlassFish installation: components that are currently installed in the GlassFish instance, and available repositories from which additional GlassFish components can be searched for and installed. For the open source distribution of the GlassFish Server, two default repositories are configured, and they are identified with the prefix `dev.glassfish.org` and `contrib.glassfish.org` respectively.

Using the update tool utilities

GlassFish provides two versions of the update tool to interact with the IPS – a standalone version and a web-based version integrated into the GlassFish Admin Console. Both versions have the same essential functionality, except that the standalone version does not need the GlassFish Server to be running, and it has an update notifier that can be configured to automatically check for updates. Finally, the standalone update tool allows us to manage the update of multiple GlassFish 3 installations on the same server.

To access the integrated update tool, simply log on to the Admin Console, and click the **Update Tool** node in the navigation panel. The user interface of this update tool is shown in the following screenshot.

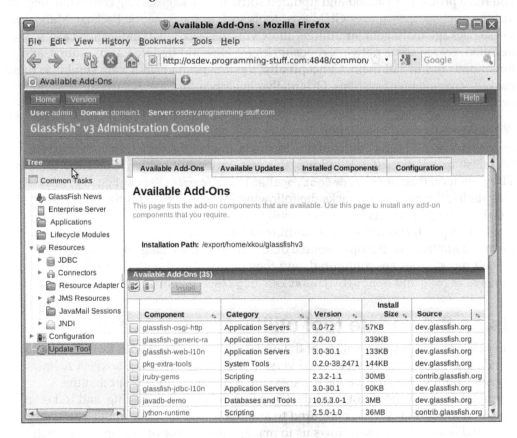

The update tool user interface is very straightforward. By navigating through different tabs, you should be able to quickly learn how to install, remove, and update software packages for your GlassFish instance.

About the standalone update tool

To launch the standalone update tool, we can start it with the following commands:

```
# cd $AS_INSTALL/bin
# ./updatetool
```

The **Update Tool** interface is shown in the following screenshot.

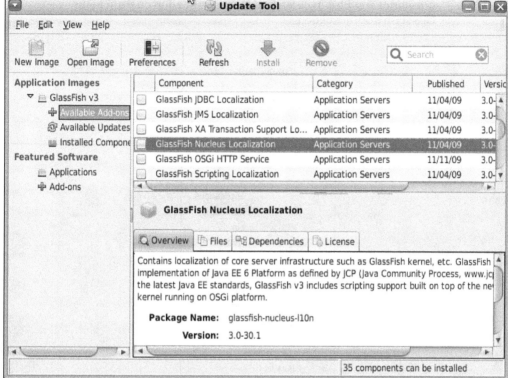

Using the update tool, we can easily discover update packages available for the GlassFish 3 installation, select them, and install them. This can significantly reduce the efforts required for the application server maintenance.

Exploring the GlassFish directory structure

The essential directory structure under `$AS_INSTALL` directory of the GlassFish installation is illustrated in the following screenshot. The purpose and content of these directories is discussed in the following section.

The installer-based GlassFish distribution also creates several additional directories and files. You can find more information on them in the GlassFish documentation.

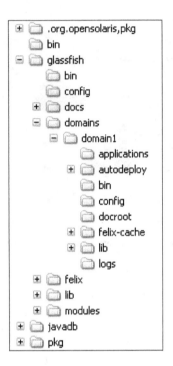

If you have experience with previous versions of GlassFish, the **glassfish** directory should look very familiar. It is the GlassFish Server instance directory, which contains the server configuration, runtime libraries and deployed applications, and so on. Compared to previous versions of GlassFish (v1 and v2), a noticeable difference in GlassFish 3 is that the server runtime libraries are stored in the **modules**, instead of **lib** directory. Furthermore, the runtime libraries are split into individual archives. This is due to the modular design of GlassFish 3, where the server runtime is composed of the needed modules only.

The directory **javadb** contains a distribution of the Java DB database system based on the Apache Derby project. Java DB provides a small and pure Java implementation of a **Relational Database System (RDBMS)**. It can be used as an embedded persistent and relational data store. In fact, the GlassFish timer service and call flow monitoring features both use the embedded Java DB for data storage. Java DB is also suitable for prototyping and small scale deployment.

The **bin** directory contains three important executable scripts for the GlassFish: asadmin, pkg and updatetool. You have used asadmin to start and stop the GlassFish Server earlier in the chapter, and a detailed discussion of the capability of asadmin will be given in the next chapter.

The other two scripts in the bin directory, pkg and updatetool and other directories in the GlassFish installation directories are related to the update tool utilities of GlassFish. As the update tool utility plays an essential role in administering the GlassFish Server, in the next section, let's understand its features and functionality and see how we can use it.

 For the full GlassFish 3 installation, the OpenMQ is also installed, and it is installed in the mq directory.

The structure of the default domain: domain1

The directory structure of the default domain, domain1 is illustrated in the following screenshot:

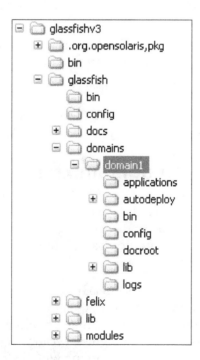

The highlighted directory, **domain1** corresponds to the domain root directory for **domain1**. In GlassFish, each domain corresponds to a directory with the same name as the domain. By default, all the domains are created under the domain root directory $AS_INSTALL/glassfish/domains.

The content of each directory under **domain1** is described as follows:

- The **applications** directory contains Java EE applications deployed to the GlassFish Server.

- The **autodeploy** directory allows you to automatically deploy applications by simply copying the application archive file to this directory.

- The **lib** directory contains directories that contribute to the class path of the domain and applications deployed to it. It also contains an embedded Java DB database that is used as the default data store for the EJB timer service.

- The **config** directory contains all the configuration files for the domain. It is critical to have a good understanding of these files to be able to administer and configure the GlassFish Server.

- The **bin** directory is empty for the GlassFish 3 prelude distribution. Historically, this directory contained the native scripts to stop and start server instance.

- The **docroot** directory contains the default static content. Upon installation, there is only one file, index.html representing the default page for GlassFish.

- The **logs** directory contains the GlassFish Server log files.

Now let's examine the **config** directory more closely to get familiar with the essential configuration files for the domain.

Getting familiar with domain.xml

First, unlike previous versions of the GlassFish Server where the schema of the domain.xml is defined by an XML DTD, GlassFish 3 no longer has a DTD for domain.xml. Instead, the structure of the domain.xml file is determined by the Java API that makes up the configuration part of the GlassFish administration infrastructure discussed in next section.

The high-level element hierarchy of the domain.xml file is illustrated in the following figure. In this figure, unless explicitly noted, the multiplicity of child elements is many. For example, the application element may contain multiple engine elements. The config element in the figure is highlighted because of its complexity. In fact, the rest of this book more or less focuses on working with the config element, such as tuning the GlassFish Server and configuring different types of services.

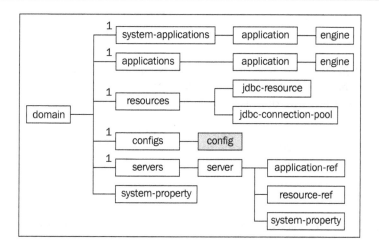

The root element of the hierarchy, domain defines a GlassFish administrative domain. The top level child elements of domain are described as follows:

- The system-applications and applications elements describe the applications deployed in the GlassFish Server. Technically, there is no difference between a system application and a normal application. However, in practice, system applications are bundled with the GlassFish Server, such as the Admin Console web application. On the other hand, applications you developed and deployed to GlassFish are typically considered as normal applications. Each deployed application is described by a distinct application element. The engine child element of application is used to specify appropriate sniffers to identify the type of the application, and appropriate containers and services that should be used to run the application.

- The resources element describes resources configured for the domain, such as JDBC connection pools and data sources.

- The configs element contains one or multiple config element. Each config element defines a collection of services and other settings. These services together define the behavior of a runtime server instance.

- The servers element contains one or multiple server elements. Each server element defines a server instance. Each server element contains an attribute that provides a reference to a config defined in the domain. xml file. Furthermore, the server element uses its resources-ref and application-ref elements to identify necessary applications and resources to be supported by the server instance at runtime.

- Finally, the `system-property` element can be applied to `domain`, `server`, and `config` elements. A `system-property` element essentially defines a variable in the corresponding scope, (from high to low levels, domain, server or config), and the value of this property can be referenced using the notation `${prop-name}`. Furthermore, a system property defined at a lower level can overwrite the value defined at a higher level.

With this introduction, we hope you got a good understanding of the high-level structure of GlassFish 3. We also hope that you got a good first impression on similarities and differences between GlassFish 3 and GlassFish 2, and hopefully you saw that a lot of experience we got from working with GlassFish 2 can be easily transferred to GlassFish 3.

In the next section, let's go through an overview of the administrative utilities of GlassFish 3.

Administering GlassFish 3

In this section, we discuss the utilities that help us perform these tasks. Similar to GlassFish 2, we can administer GlassFish 3 using these two utilities:

- The Admin Console: A browser-based tool that allows you to perform administrative tasks using the web interface.

- The `asadmin` CLI utility: A command-line tool that allows you to perform most administrative tasks from a command terminal.

Both tools can perform similar configuration changes, with the `asadmin` utility incorporating slightly more functionality.

Using the Admin Console

The look and feel of the GlassFish 3 Admin Console is very similar to that of GlassFish 2. The main differences are the following:

- The integrated update tool in GlassFish 3.

- The structure of the **Configuration** node is shown in the following screenshot. In this screenshot, the **Ruby Container** node allows us to configure the Ruby container for deployed Ruby-on-Rails applications, and the **Network Config** node gives us more control of the Grizzly connector implementations compared to GlassFish 2.

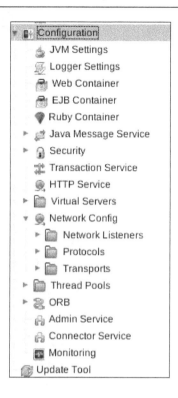

Using the asadmin CLI utility

Located in the $AS_INSTALL/bin directory, the asadmin CLI utility has been improved to provide more capability in GlassFish 3. You can enter the following command to view the help page of the asadmin utility:

```
# cd $AS_INSTALL/bin
# ./asadmin  help | more
```

There are two types of subcommands. Local subcommands can be run without a running domain administration server (DAS). However, you must have access to the installation directory and the domain directory. Remote subcommands are always run by connecting to a DAS. You can view a list of subcommands supported by asadmin with the following command:

```
# cd $AS_INSTALL/bin
# ./asadmin list-commands
```

The output of the `list-commands` lists both local and remote commands, as shown in the following sample output:

```
********** Local Commands **********
create-domain
delete-domain
list-commands
list-domains
login
monitor
start-database
start-domain
stop-database
stop-domain
version
********** Remote Commands **********
__locations                          disable
add-resources                        enable
change-admin-password                generate-jvm-report
create-audit-module                  get
create-auth-realm                    list
create-file-user                     list-applications
create-http-listener                 list-audit-modules
create-jdbc-connection-pool          list-auth-realms
create-jdbc-resource                 list-commands
create-jvm-options                   list-components
create-message-security-provider     list-containers
create-password-alias                list-file-groups
create-profiler                      list-file-users
create-resource-ref                  list-http-listeners
create-ssl                           list-jdbc-connection-pools
create-system-properties             list-jdbc-resources
create-virtual-server                list-jvm-options
delete-audit-module                  list-message-security-providers
delete-auth-realm                    list-modules
delete-file-user                     list-password-aliases
delete-http-listener                 list-resource-refs
delete-jdbc-connection-pool          list-system-properties
```

```
delete-jdbc-resource              list-virtual-servers
delete-jvm-options                monitor
delete-message-security-provider  ping-connection-pool
delete-password-alias             redeploy
delete-profiler                   set
delete-resource-ref               stop-domain
delete-ssl                        undeploy
delete-system-property            update-file-user
delete-virtual-server             update-password-alias
deploy                            uptime
deploydir                         version
```

Different commands may have different options and operands. The best way to learn the syntax of each sub-command is by running the following command:

```
# cd $AS_INSTALL/bin
# ./asadmin <subcommand> --help
```

This command displays detailed help information for the subcommand. For example, if you want to know how to run the list-commands subcommand, you can enter the following commands from a terminal:

```
# cd $AS_INSTALL/bin
# ./asadmin list-commands -help |more
```

The first several lines of the output print the synopsis of the subcommand, for example:

```
list-commands
[--terse={true|false}] [ --echo={true|false} ]
[ --interactive={true|false} ] [ --host  host]
[--port port] [--secure| -s ] [ --user  admin_user]
[--passwordfile filename] [--help]
[--localonly ={false|true}] [--remoteonly ={false|true}]
```

This output explains the options the subcommand accepts. Many options have a long form and a short form. For example, the long option --terse can be written in the form of -t.

Using the the HTTP interface of the asadmin utility

Starting from GlassFish 3, you can access the remote commands of the `asadmin` utility in a RESTful fashion. For example, you can open a browser, and access the following URL: `http://localhost:4848/__asadmin/list-containers`. This command tries to list all the application containers currently configured for the GlassFish Server.

The output is shown in the following screenshot. Except for formatting, the output is actually the same as if you are running the following commands from a terminal:

```
# cd $AS_INSTALL/bin
# ./asadmin list-containers
```

The HTTP interface for the `asadmin` utility makes it even easier to administer the GlassFish Server.

Working with GlassFish containers

As a fully Java EE compliant application server, GlassFish implements all the mandatory containers for Java EE application components. In previous version of the GlassFish Server, the server software distribution always includes all the containers. GlassFish 3 no longer follows this monolithic approach, and its container architecture is highly dynamic and flexible. In GlassFish 3, the Web container, EJB container, and **Message Driven Bean** (**MDB**) containers are bundled as separate modules. These modules can be dynamically added to or removed from the GlassFish Server using the updatetool or the IPS package management utility, pkg.

In addition, GlassFish implements a container for Ruby on Rails applications. For example, the following command installs the JRuby container and the previous configured Ruby on Rails gems.

```
# pkg install jruby jruby-gems
```

When the GlassFish Server is running, we can use the list-containers command of the asadmin CLI to check the containers currently installed on the GlassFish Server. For example:

```
# cd $AS_INSTALL/bin
# ./asadmin list-containers
```

The output of the command should be similar to the following:

```
List all known application containers
Container : grizzly
Container : web
Container : ear
Container : security
Container : ejb
Container : weld
Container : osgi
Container : webservices
Container : jpa
Container : connector
Container : appclient
Container : jruby
Command list-containers executed successfully.
```

As we can see, GlassFish 3 uses the container architecture to provide the support for many popular application frameworks and languages. Depending on the application we need to host, you can install and remove these containers to tailor the GlassFish Server.

When different containers modules are added or removed, the Admin Console of GlassFish makes synchronized changes by providing or removing the Admin Console user interface corresponding to the feature.

This pluggable architecture of the GlassFish container has the following advantages:

- It reduces the server footprint by not installing unused containers.
- It allows the GlassFish Server to be tailored for specific applications, thus providing a better chance for performance tuning.
- We can build other additional container modules to extend the GlassFish Server.

The last feature is particularly appealing. In fact, GlassFish uses a container model to provide direct support for the popular Rails web application framework running on JRuby. By doing this, Rails applications takes advantage of the high performance of the Grizzly NIO network framework and the multi-threaded runtime environment of the GlassFish Server. Furthermore, multiple Rails applications can be deployed to one GlassFish Server installation.

Embedded GlassFish

Most applications deployed to GlassFish run in the aforementioned "hosting" mode, where multiple applications are deployed to one server installation. It is also possible to use embedded GlassFish to support different applications. In this "embedded" mode, a minimized configuration of GlassFish, including appropriate container and service modules are bundled within an application's distribution, and GlassFish provides a dedicated lightweight runtime environment for the application.

Examples of embedded GlassFish include the JRuby and Grails modules for GlassFish. We will show you later in this chapter that these applications can be deployed to a hosting server, or uses its dedicated embedded GlassFish Server.

In our experience, the embedded mode of GlassFish application support is useful during development, because it makes the development environment very small and easy to manage. The embedded mode can also be useful when the application has some very specific functionality, and the application does not induce a high level of concurrency.

Deploying applications to GlassFish 3

In this section, we discuss the application deployment features of GlassFish, and then introduce the tools we use to deploy and configure applications.

Application deployment features

The application deployment features are explained in the following sections.

Directory based deployment

Traditionally the most common mechanism to deploy a Java EE application is to create an appropriate archive file, such as a WAR file for web applications, and then deploy the archive to the application server. Besides this standard deployment approach, GlassFish also allows you to deploy an application in its exploded directory structure (directory deployment), as long as you specify where the server can load the application from upon deployment.

 According to the GlassFish documentation, if you are deploying a directory on a mapped drive in Windows, the user running the GlassFish Server must be the same user who assigned the mapped drive. Otherwise, GlassFish cannot see the directory.

Dynamic reload and automatic deployment support

GlassFish supports dynamic deployment of applications. With dynamic deployment, you do not need to restart the server with a deployment, redeploy or undeploy. Furthermore, you do not have to redeploy a module when you change its code or deployment descriptors. For example, when you compile some new classes or change the deployment descriptors, you can simply copy the changed files into the deployment directory for the module. After this, you can run a touch command to modify the time stamp of the file reload within the application's root top level directory. The server checks for changes periodically and redeploys the module, automatically and dynamically, with the changes.

Dynamic reloading is useful in development. However, the periodic change check done by the server can impact the overall server performance. Due to this, in a production environment this feature should be turned off.

 Dynamic reload is enabled to true by default.

GlassFish 3 implements the **Keep Sessions** feature that allows the HTTP sessions to be kept alive when an application is redeployed. This could significantly improve the development and testing productivity. Keep in mind that these features are mostly developer oriented. In production environments, application deployment should be done with caution.

 By default, the **Keep Session** feature is disabled.

GlassFish also supports automatic deployment. By default, when you copy an application archive file to the `$domain_dir/autodeploy` directory, GlassFish will automatically load the application and deploy it. To undeploy an automatically deployed module, just remove the file from the `autodeploy` directory.

Configuring application libraries

If multiple application modules require the same libraries, we can factor out these common libraries, store them in a shared directory, and simply refer to the shared libraries when you deploy the application. This feature allows you to reduce the size of application modules.

Application deployment tools on GlassFish

You can use the `asadmin` command-line utility or the Admin Console to deploy applications.

 Technically, these two utilities should provide comparable capabilities. Currently, however, the Admin Console deployment is rather limited. Since the Admin Console does not properly integrate with different application containers and modules in the GlassFish 3 Prelude release, the only application you can deploy using the Admin console are Java EE web modules.

Using the asadmin CLI utility

The following commands of the `asadmin` utility allow you to manage application deployment:

- `deploy`: Deploy an application module. If the module is already deployed, you can force redeployment by setting the `--force` option to true. You can also deploy a module in an expanded directory structure.

- `redeploy`: Redeploys an application module. Whenever redeployment is done, the sessions at that transit time become invalid unless you use the `keepSessions=true` property of the `asadmin redeploy` command.

- `undeploy`: Undeploys a web or EJB module.

- `disable`: Immediately disables a web or EJB module. Disabling a web module makes it inaccessible to clients.

- `enable`: Immediately enables a web or EJB module.

- `list-components`: Lists all deployed modules and their containers.

Using the Admin Console

The application deployment user interface of the Admin Console is shown in the following screenshot. When we click the **Deploy** button, we can choose to upload an application archive file, or specify the location of the application where GlassFish 3 has access. Note that in this case the application can be in an archived form, or in an exploded form with the appropriate directory structure.

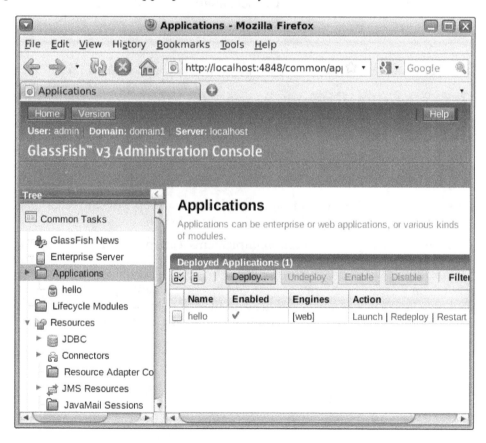

Application deployment tutorial

This section shows you how to deploy the following types of application:

- Java EE Web application and JAX-WS web service endpoints
- RESTful web services implemented in JAX-RS
- Ruby on Rails applications that runs in JRuby
- Grails applications

Several simple applications are provided to you, and you can find them in the `$samples/g3` directory. We assume you are relatively familiar with Java EE applications, such as web components and web services. All the sample applications provided with this book were developed using the NetBeans IDE. If you are not familiar with the technical details of these applications, we encourage you to explore the source code of the applications.

In the following tutorials, we will use the command-line interface, and when necessary, we should use the Admin Console interface that allows us to achieve the same goal.

Working with Java EE web applications and web services

In this section, we will show you how to deploy and configure the following simple web applications:

- `SimpleWS`: This web application implements a simple JAX-WS web service endpoint that is consumed by the `SimpleWeb` application.
- `SimpleWeb`: This web application implements a couple of simple JSP pages to invoke the `SimpleWS` web service, and renders the event.
- `SimpleRS`: This web application implements a simple RESTful web service implemented in JAX-RS.

In order to run these applications, you should have the following modules installed on GlassFish: Metro web service and the Jersey implementation of the JAX-RS specification. To check if you have the Metro module installed, enter the following commands:

```
# cd $AS_INSTALL/bin
# ./pkg list
```

If Metro is installed, the output should report the version of the modules. Otherwise, you will need to install it with the following command:

```
# ./pkg install metro jersey
```

> Note that if you install multiple modules using the pkg utility, simply separate the module names with whitespace. Also, if you install the module using the Admin Console, you can log on to the console, click **Updatetool**, select the **Available Addons** panel, select **Metro**, and click **Install**.

Once you have installed Metro, enter the following commands to deploy the application:

```
# cd $AS_INSTALL/bin
# ./asadmin deploy $samples/g3/SimpleWS/dist/SimpleWS.war
# ./asadmin deploy $samples/g3/SimpleWeb/dist/SimpleWeb.war
# ./asadmin deploy $samples/g3/SimpleRS/dist/SimpleRS.war
```

You can verify the deployment of these applications as follows:

- For the SimpleWeb web service application, you can access the following URL to test it: http://localhost:8080/SimpleWS/SimpleWSService?Tester. The tester page has a simple user interface that allows you to provide request parameter values, as shown in the following screenshot.

- For the `SimpleWeb` application, you can verify it by accessing the URL `http://localhost:8080/SimpleWeb/webservice.jsp`. The `webservice.jsp` page accepts the user input, and passes the parameter to invoke the `SimpleWS` web service.

- To verify the `SimpleRS` RESTful service, access the URL `http://localhost:8080/SimpleRS/resources/rest`. You should see a simple response like the following:

  Hello, this is a RESTful service.

> For more information on JAX-WS, JAX-RS, you can visit the following websites: `https://metro.dev.java.net`, and `https://jersey.dev.java.net`. Also, the Java EE Tutorial book downloadable from Sun Microsystem website `http://java.sun.com/javaee/5/docs/tutorial/doc` provides an excellent introduction to the programming model.

Working with JRuby and Rails applications

The GlassFish Server provides excellent support for running Ruby on Rails (RoR) web applications using the JRuby container. This section first provides a brief introduction to RoR, and then shows you how to use GlassFish to run RoR applications in both the hosting and embedded mode.

JRuby on Rails and GlassFish 3

Support for the JRuby on Rails applications in GlassFish is excellent, and some features are described here:

- Rails applications can be deployed to GlassFish as a directory or a web archive.
- One GlassFish instance can host multiple Rails web applications.
- Rails application can be configured to use a thread pool to handle concurrent requests.
- Rails application can also use a dedicated and embedded GlassFish 3 Server to serve requests.

Now let's see how to support JRuby on Rails applications on GlassFish. In this tutorial, we will use a simple JRuby on Rails application to demonstrate how to configure GlassFish. The application is located in `<sample-dir>/deploy/SimpleRails`.

The sample application requires a MySQL database backend. In this chapter, we will focus on configuring data sources and other resources in details.

Deploying JRuby on Rails application to GlassFish

In order to deploy Rails applications, GlassFish must have a JRuby runtime container. The easiest way to install and configure JRuby is to use the `pkg` utility:

```
# pkg install jruby jruby-gems
```

This command will install the JRuby at `$AS_INSTALL/glassfish/modules/jruby`, and it also installs the Rails and several JDBC gems that allow you to use JDBC connections to enable active record-based persistence.

You can also use your own JRuby installation to provide the JRuby support on GlassFish. In order to do this, complete the following instructions:

1. Download the JRuby binary from `http://jruby.org`.

2. Extract the JRuby binary to a directory. Lets call it `<JRUBY_HOME>`.

3. Enter the following commands to install the necessary Ruby gems:

   ```
   # cd $JRUBY_HOME

   # bin/jruby -S gem install rails activerecord-jdbc-adapter
   activerecord-jdbcmysql-adapter jdbc-mysql warbler
   ```

4. Edit `$AS_INSTALL/domains/domain1/config/domain.xml` and add this entry inside element:

   ```
   <java-config>
     <jvm-options>-Djruby.home=$JRUBY_HOME</jvm-options>
   </java-config>
   ```

5. Restart GlassFish Server.

Once JRuby is configured, complete the following steps to deploy the sample `SimpleRails` application:

1. Edit the `database.yml` file in `<sample-dir>/deploy/SimplRails/config` to point to the MySQL server you can access.

2. Enter the follow command to run the database migration:

   ```
   # cd $samples/g3/SimplRails

   # $JRUBY_HOME/bin/jruby -S rake db:migrate
   ```

3. Enter the following command to deploy the application:

```
# cd $AS_INSTALL/bin
# ./asadmin deploy $samples/g3/SimplRails
```

4. Once the application is deployed, you can verify it by accessing the URL:
   `http://localhost:8080/SimpleRails/posts`.

The application's interface is shown in the following screenshot. This simple application allows you to create, edit, and delete posts.

The aforementioned method performs a directory-based deployment of the Rails application to GlassFish. You can also use the warbler gem to create a self-container WAR file of the application, and deploy the WAR file. To do that, enter the following commands:

```
# cd $samples/g3/SimpleRails
# $JRUBY_HOME/bin/jruby -S warble
```

Once the command finishes, the `SimpleRails` WAR file is created under the `SimpleRails` application directory. You can deploy this WAR file just like a web application.

Configuring Rails thread pools

One of the big advantages of using JRuby for Rails application is that multiple Rails runtime instances (thread pool) can be created, thus potentially improving the performance and throughput of the application. GlassFish allows you to configure the JRuby runtime environment with the following elements in the GlassFish `domain.xml` configuration file, located in `<AS-INSTALL>/glassfish/domains/domain1/config`:

```
<java-config>
  <jvm-options>-Djruby.runtime.min=1</jvm-options>
  <jvm-options>-Djruby.runtime=2</jvm-options>
  <jvm-options>-Djruby.runtime.max=3</jvm-options>
</java-config>
```

The properties of the above elements are explained as follows:

- `-Djruby.runtime=X` sets the initial number of JRuby runtimes that GlassFish starts with. The default value is 1. This represents the highest value that GlassFish accepts as minimum runtimes, and the lowest value that GlassFish uses as maximum runtimes.

- `-Djruby.runtime.max=X` sets the maximum number of JRuby runtimes that might be available in the pool. The default value is 2. For this element, too high values might result in OutOfMemory errors, either in the heap or in the PermGen.

- `-Djruby.runtime.min=X` sets the minimum number of JRuby runtimes that will be available in the pool. The default value is one. The pool will always be at least this large, but can be larger than this.

The dynamic runtime pool maintains itself with the minimum number of runtimes possible, to allow consistent and fast runtime access for the requesting application. The pool may take an initial runtime value, but that value is not used after pool creation.

Running Rails application with embedded GlassFish

The embedded version of the Glassfish 3 is available as a Ruby gem. If you install this gem on top of the JRuby installation, you can use Glassfish as an embedded web server to render the Rails application.

To install the glassfish gem, enter the following commands:

```
# cd $JRUBY_HOME
# bin/jruby -S gem install glassfish
```

Once the gem is installed, you can use the embedded GlassFish Server to run the application with the following commands:

```
# cd $samples/g3
# jruby -S rails SimpleRails
```

To access the application, access the following URL: `http://localhost:3000/posts`.

The `SimpleRails` application should appear. Note that in this case, the embedded GlassFish is listening on port 3000, not 8080.

Working with Grails applications

Grails is another popular web application framework written in the Groovy programming language. Grails is similar to Rails, it is also based on MVC architecture, and it also has a persistence layer for object-relational mapping (using the Hibernate open source project). Also, the Groovy programming language is dynamic, and it has a similar syntax with Ruby. However, because it was built as a programming language for the Java Virtual Machine (JVM) from ground up, the Groovy programming language has a more straightforward integration with the Java language. Due to this, many Java developers have found that the Grails framework is easier to use than Rails.

The support for Grails and GlassFish is similar to that for Rails in the following ways:

- Grails application can run in hosted or embedded mode
- Grails support is based on the GlassFish Grails container module

Now let's look at how the Grails applications are supported.

Running Grails application with embedded GlassFish

The Grails module available in the GlassFish repository has an embedded GlassFish as the web server. Once you create a Grails application and use the GlassFish Grails module to run it, the application is rendered by the embedded GlassFish.

For example, the following steps show you how to enable Grails deployment for `SimpleGroovy`:

- First, install the Grails module:

  ```
  # cd $AS_INSTALL/bin
  # ./pgk install grails
  ```

- Next, set the `GRAILS_HOME` environment variable to point to the Grails module installed in GlassFish:

  ```
  # export GRAILS_HOME=$AS_INSTALL/glassfish/grails
  # export PATH=$GRAILS_HOME/grails:$PATH
  ```

- Change the directory to `<sample-dir>/deploy/SimpleGroovy/grails-app/conf`, and modify the `DataSource.groovy` to point to an accessible MySQL database.

- Start the application with the following commands:

  ```
  # cd $sample/g3/SimpleGroovy
  # grails run-app
  ```

Once the application starts, access the URL: `http://localhost:8080/SimpleGroovy/post`. The application should look like the following screenshot:

Deploying Grails applications to GlassFish

Traditionally, Grails applications can always be assembled into a WAR file so they can be deployed as a web application. However, the WAR file created was large. GlassFish 3 improved this by taking advantage of the application shared library feature. The following steps demonstrate how to do this.

First, set the environment variables for Grails:

```
# export GRAILS_HOME=$AS_INSTALL/glassfish/grails
# export PATH=$GRAILS_HOME/grails:$PATH
```

Now, create the WAR file using the `shared-war` task:

```
# cd $samples/g3/SimpleGroovy
# grails shared-war
```

Once the command finishes, the `Simplegroovy-0.1.war` is created under the application directory.

Now deploy the application:

```
# $AS_INSTALL/bin/asadmin deploy --libraries $GRAILS_HOME/lib/glassfish-
grails.jar SimpleGroovy-0.1.war
```

Summary

This chapter provides an overview of the upcoming GlassFish 3. We focused on the new features of GlassFish 3, and how to install and administer GlassFish 3, and how to deploy applications to the server. We did not discuss several topics such as resource and security configuration. The reasons for this are:

- Along the development timeline of GlasssFish 3, support for configuring different resources and security features was gradually added in later builds of GlassFish.

- For most of the resource and security features that are implemented in the current GlassFish 3 builds, there administration and configuration is actually very similar to GlassFish 2.

Due to this, we strongly recommend you use this chapter as a starting point, and refer to the GlassFish 3 website and documentation for more up-to-date coverage on these topics.

Index

Symbols

A

Thank you for buying
GlassFish Administration

Packt Open Source Project Royalties

When we sell a book written on an Open Source project, we pay a royalty directly to that project. Therefore by purchasing GlassFish Administration, Packt will have given some of the money received to the GlassFish project.

In the long term, we see ourselves and you—customers and readers of our books—as part of the Open Source ecosystem, providing sustainable revenue for the projects we publish on. Our aim at Packt is to establish publishing royalties as an essential part of the service and support a business model that sustains Open Source.

If you're working with an Open Source project that you would like us to publish on, and subsequently pay royalties to, please get in touch with us.

Writing for Packt

We welcome all inquiries from people who are interested in authoring. Book proposals should be sent to author@packtpub.com. If your book idea is still at an early stage and you would like to discuss it first before writing a formal book proposal, contact us; one of our commissioning editors will get in touch with you.

We're not just looking for published authors; if you have strong technical skills but no writing experience, our experienced editors can help you develop a writing career, or simply get some additional reward for your expertise.

About Packt Publishing

Packt, pronounced 'packed', published its first book "Mastering phpMyAdmin for Effective MySQL Management" in April 2004 and subsequently continued to specialize in publishing highly focused books on specific technologies and solutions.

Our books and publications share the experiences of your fellow IT professionals in adapting and customizing today's systems, applications, and frameworks. Our solution-based books give you the knowledge and power to customize the software and technologies you're using to get the job done. Packt books are more specific and less general than the IT books you have seen in the past. Our unique business model allows us to bring you more focused information, giving you more of what you need to know, and less of what you don't.

Packt is a modern, yet unique publishing company, which focuses on producing quality, cutting-edge books for communities of developers, administrators, and newbies alike. For more information, please visit our website: www.PacktPub.com.

Java EE 5 Development using GlassFish Application Server

ISBN: 978-1-847192-60-8   Paperback: 424 pages

The complete guide to installing and configuring the GlassFish Application Server and developing Java EE 5 applications to be deployed to this server

1. Concise guide covering all major aspects of Java EE 5 development

2. Uses the enterprise open-source GlassFish application server

3. Explains GlassFish installation and configuration

Java EE 5 Development with NetBeans 6

ISBN: 978-1-847195-46-3   Paperback: 400 pages

Develop professional enterprise Java EE applications quickly and easily with this popular IDE

1. Use features of the popular NetBeans IDE to improve Java EE development

2. Careful instructions and screenshots lead you through the options available

3. Covers the major Java EE APIs such as JSF, EJB 3 and JPA, and how to work with them in NetBeans

Please check **www.PacktPub.com** for information on our titles

EJB 3 Developer Guide

ISBN: 978-1-847195-60-9   Paperback: 276 pages

A Practical Guide for developers and architects to the Enterprise Java Beans Standard.

1. A rapid introduction to the features of EJB 3

2. EJB 3 features explored concisely with accompanying code examples

3. Easily enhance Java applications with new, improved Enterprise Java Beans

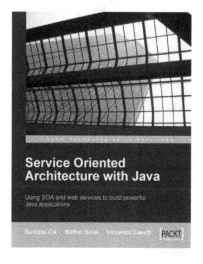

Service Oriented Architecture with Java

ISBN: 978-1-847193-21-6   Paperback: 192 pages

Using SOA and web services to build powerful Java applications

1. Build effective SOA applications with Java Web Services

2. Quick reference guide with best-practice design examples

3. Understand SOA concepts from core with examples

4. Design scalable inter-enterprise communication

9 781847 196507